ACCIDENTAL SAFARI

A guide for navigating the
challenges that come with aging

RICHARD C. TIZZANO

Accidental Safari: *A guide for navigating the challenges that come with aging.*
Richard Tizzano © 2017

Print ISBN: 978-0-9995819-0-2
eBook ISBN: 978-0-9995819-1-9

Cover Design & Footprint Graphic: Bonnie Dickson
Interior Layout & Design: Fusion Creative Works, FusionCW.com

First Printing
Printed in the United States of America

Richard Tizzano speaks regularly and can be contacted at (360)779-5551
or at richardt@legalpeaceofmind.com or www.accidentalsafari.com

To my wife, wow, thank you for your love
and enduring support. Proverbs 31

To my six wonderful children who work
tirelessly to stretch me into who
God wants me to be.

CONTENTS

1: THE CIRCLE OF LIFE 15

We end life as we began it, needing essential care. Every one of us hopes to be healthy and active in body, mind, and spirit for as long as possible, but most of us will face an Accidental Safari sometime in our lifetime.

2: A STRUGGLE FOR SURVIVAL 25

As we age, there are threats that can sneak up on us. Accidents and disorders of the brain and body are the primary causes of hospitalization and death for the elderly.

3: THE ROAD MOST TAKEN 37

Understanding the path of the long-term care journey will help you anticipate and prepare for the challenges ahead. Expecting the unexpected increases your options.

PREFACE

"Safari" (Swahili; N.): A journey

Accidental Safari describes the intimate adventure of giving and receiving care that we all experience as we age. It weaves together stories from my own life with stories of "Accidental Safaris" shared by clients and friends through my practice as an elder law attorney. I have changed the names of these clients and friends to protect their anonymity, but their stories are true accounts of experiences they encountered following an unexpected health crisis. This book was written to share vital information about the tools you will need to survive and thrive during an Accidental Safari of your own.

I grew up in a multi-generational home in Queens, New York. My parents rented the second-floor apartment in my grandparents' home prior to the 1965 Social Security Act Amendments signed by President Lyndon Johnson. These amendments created Medicare and Medicaid and changed the way America cared for its elderly. Medicaid guaranteed payment for the cost of care in a nursing home for those unable to pay for care. This guarantee of payment created the nursing home industry. In most countries around the world, the elderly are cared for by family members at home.

My father, who was 47 years of age when my mother was paralyzed by a stroke, took care of her for the rest of her life. He demonstrated to me what it means to be content in any and all circumstances. He also modeled a determination never to quit. My grandparents, aunts, and uncles showed the same resolve and compassion. The entire family rallied around my father and me as we cared for my mother. My exposure to old fashioned, loving, in-home care turned my young heart to the needs of the elderly. I learned the skills and tricks necessary to survive, and even thrive, when a loved one needs 24/7 care. The challenges we faced together as a family and our joy in the process enriched my childhood significantly and gave life a richer and deeper meaning.

My mother's stroke also led to a personal epiphany. I had the stunning realization that although there was pain in the world, I could be a force for good by running toward, not away from, the challenges of being a caregiver. I learned the truth that giving care is a privilege that brings a blessing. These experiences planted the seed that has become my life's work—helping others through their own Accidental Safari.

Over the past twenty-five years, as the Baby Boomer generation has grown older, the elder law part of my practice has grown exponentially. Many of these clients have sought my help in response to unplanned health emergencies that required immediate attention. In each situation, it was as if a family member had been abducted and sent on a frightening and perilous journey. Families faced with unexpected expenses in the thousands or even tens of thousands of dollars every month were looking for immediate answers and financial relief. They were looking for someone who could help guide them safely out of the jungle. They were looking for hope.

Sadly, many of the people I met with could have avoided much of the pain of the unexpected health crisis if they had spent time planning ahead for an Accidental Safari. I came to realize that if I could help people see that the light they thought they were seeing at the end of the tunnel was actually an oncoming train, they might act sooner. I began to offer free public seminars to issue the warning. People came. After two years, my practice began to change. Today, I am seeing fewer emergencies. I like to think that, in some small way, I have helped to develop an increasing awareness of the issues related to aging and this, in turn, is reducing the number of emergencies. I find it gratifying to help people work through these issues and develop a plan before a crisis occurs.

An Accidental Safari can happen to any one of us. This book can help you prepare, so you can make the most of the adventure when it comes. I hope it will serve as a guide and a source of hope in the midst of possible despair.

Life will one day come to an end for each of us. But the end can be as purposeful and meaningful as the beginning and the middle. It is my wish that this book will provide you with practical steps and information to prepare you for an Accidental Safari and bring you physical, financial, and spiritual peace. May you live well and end well.

INTRODUCTION

Many people recognize the importance of planning for retirement. They develop an estate plan and create a budget. Some also purchase long-term healthcare insurance. They feel well prepared for the future. But these people may one day find themselves in a crisis they didn't plan for. An accident or unexpected medical diagnosis suddenly thrusts them into hostile and unfamiliar territory. They find themselves, or someone they care about, trapped by circumstances entirely beyond their control. They are completely unprepared for the onslaught of immediate and complex medical issues and decisions they must make. It's as though they have been kidnapped and sent on a sudden and unplanned Safari against their will. They would never have elected to take this "Accidental Safari," but they were not given a choice. Without warning, they are now in a fight for survival.

Whether it's your journey or you are the advocate for someone else on this Safari, the shock and the fear of traveling this unfamiliar path can be crippling. The good news is that the paths through this jungle have been heavily traveled and are predictable. Because they are predictable, they can be anticipated and, if they can be anticipated, you can be prepared.

This book is not intended to be a substitute for the counsel of professional financial, medical, and legal advisors who are attuned to your individual circumstances and needs. However, if you or a loved one have found yourselves on an unexpected health journey, this book can be your guide to the options that remain to you when your "normal" has been stripped away. Just as a traveler needs a map, this book will light a path for you through unknown territory. It will help you identify the good guys from the bad guys and the poisonous plants from the edible ones. Whatever the reason you now find yourself on "Safari," be it a traumatic stroke, heart attack, accident, or the onset of a progressive disease such as Parkinson's or Alzheimer's, your world has forever changed.

> "Time is more valuable than money. You can get more money, but you cannot get more time."
>
> — Jim Rohn

1

THE CIRCLE OF LIFE

The Lion King was right. There is a circle of life, from birth to death.

When you were born, you needed someone to love you, feed you, change your diaper, and tuck you in at night. If you live long enough, you will eventually need someone to love you, feed you, change your diaper, and tuck you in at night.

I remember the day I took my infant daughter to visit my father, who was in a nursing home. He was approaching ninety years of age, and his body and mind were failing. I had the rare privilege of changing both my child's diaper and my father's diaper on the same day. As the experience was unfolding, I had the conscious thought, "I'm going to remember this day for the rest of my life," and I have.

BEGINNINGS AND ENDINGS

Life will eventually circle around and bring us back to our beginnings, where we again need someone to provide us with essential care. A client once told me that he would like to "die young, at an old age," to be able to function at a high level right up to the time of death. The truth is, every one of us hopes to be healthy and active in body, mind, and spirit for as long as possible.

Many resources are available to instruct us on ways to delay the aging process. We can find ideas on how to think, cook (and eat), exercise, meditate, compete, help others, and travel our way to longevity. Some of these prescriptions will work for some of us, some of the time but, unfortunately, we will all run out of time eventually.

Imagine that you woke up one day and discovered that someone had deposited $86,400 into your checking account. The next morning you found that the unspent balance of yesterday's deposit had disappeared, but another $86,400 had been deposited. Imagine that this strange occurrence continued every morning. Like clockwork, the balance of the previous day's deposit was erased, and a new $86,400 was deposited. What would you do? Would you carefully and thoughtfully spend every penny every day? Or would you begin to take it for granted and leave money unspent at the end of the day?

This scenario is, in fact, what is happening each and every day to every one of us. Instead of 86,400 dollars being deposited into your bank account every morning, 86,400 seconds are being given to you! These precious seconds are yours to spend as you wish. You can spend them carefully or carelessly, but you cannot save a single second for tomorrow. As you age, the spending rate of those precious seconds seems to move ever more quickly.

The Accidental Safari begins when an accident or health crisis suddenly and unexpectedly thrusts you (or a loved one) into circumstances beyond your control. Whatever the event that begins your Safari, you now face the undeniable reality that you will need help with some of the basic activities of daily living. You need more help than you can provide for yourself.

A few years ago I found myself on a trip into central Africa—a trip that had never been on my radar screen. This "unplanned journey" started innocently enough. I was sitting in church on a Sunday morning when Carly, my ten-year-old daughter, bumped me gently with her elbow and pointed to an announcement in the weekly bulletin that read: "September 9: Informational meeting for anyone interested in a two-week mission trip to Uganda, Africa, to build a classroom for the Watoto Children's Orphanage. We will be meeting at…."

"Can we go to that meeting?" she whispered.

I read the announcement again and shrugged, "Sure."

Two weeks later, as we were sitting down for dinner, Carly said, "That meeting is tonight."

"What meeting is that?" I asked.

"You know, the one about the mission trip to Africa."

Our family had hosted children from the Watoto Children's Choir a few years earlier, so I had some frame of reference for this conversation, but a trip to Africa? I cannot imagine ever deciding to attend that "informational meeting" on my own.

When we arrived, there were about a dozen people present. It was a pleasant meeting. The mission team would raise all the money needed to buy the materials to build the classroom in Uganda as well as pay the group's travel expenses. The team would depart for Uganda in one year's time.

A light went on for me at the end of the meeting. The hostess announced the next meeting date and asked for a volunteer to bring snacks. Without a glance in my direction, for approval or encouragement, Carly raised her hand. I suddenly realized that we were going to Africa.

And so began our journey—a journey that would take a year of preparation and include vaccinations, planning meetings, work projects, shopping trips, fundraising, and rummage sales. When it was time to depart, I was confident that we were ready. To guard against the possibility of contracting malaria, my wife had literally packed six forms of mosquito repellent: DEET™ insect repellent for the deep woods, natural lemon eucalyptus pump, mosquito repellent stakes, mosquito repellent wipes, mosquito repellent bracelets, and clip-on mosquito repellent. I felt certain that we were adequately protected against malaria, but there was nothing to protect my heart and mind from the unexpected impact of the people and the culture we would meet there. Is it really possible to prepare for the unknown?

The mission trip to Uganda was something that expanded as we moved into it. It began small but ended up being much bigger in every respect than I had anticipated. It was so large, in fact, that had I known at the beginning what was going to be required of me, I'm not sure I would have begun. Looking back now, I can say that it was definitely something I would do again. The places we saw, the activities we participated in, and the friendships we made were surprising delights.

After the mission team completed the classroom, we were taken on a Safari through Queen Elizabeth National Park. The Safari was an overload to the senses: new sights, sounds, and smells; unexpected heat; and so much dust! The novelty of the experience added to my realization of just how foreign it all was and just how far away I was from all that was familiar and comfortable.

From the moment we entered the national park, we were accompanied by an experienced guide. What were my chances of survival if I had been dropped into the African wilderness alone? None; I would have died.

The truth is, we have a far better chance of survival in unfamiliar territory when we have a guide. So it is for those of us who are suddenly and unexpectedly forced to navigate the wilderness of long-term healthcare.

An Accidental Safari can be a sudden and violent abduction. The realization that you have been unwillingly forced into this unexpected journey can explode upon you without warning. Like the pounce of an unseen lion, a coronary arrest, a fall, or other major event may take you by surprise, and your only reasonable response is to dial 9-1-1. The realization of danger can also creep up on you slowly, like a venomous snake, with the onset of a progressive disease such as amyotrophic lateral sclerosis (ALS), Parkinson's disease, multiple sclerosis (MS), or chronic obstructive pulmonary disease (COPD). However the realization dawns, your life is suddenly and forever changed as you are snatched away and forced to travel this new and unforgiving landscape.

THE SAFARI BEGINS

Dialing 9-1-1 sets in motion a vast torrent of experiences, activities, events, and decisions. It is like bursting through a doorway into a different dimension where you are confronted by a world of unfamiliar sights and sounds. A new language, "medicalese," is spoken. Days and nights, devoid of your normal routines, simply run together. You find yourself in a place where a doctor, a translator, a physiologist, a shaman, a lawyer, a banker, and a guide would be extremely helpful. You discover that 9-1-1 is just the entry code into what may become a long and harrowing journey.

I have a personal memory of such an Accidental Safari: It began with my father waking me in the middle of the night. "Your mother is sick," he said. "She has to go to the hospital." A few minutes later, men in white coats arrived. As I climbed out of bed, I could see that it was just starting to grow light outside. I watched as the men rolled mother from side to side, wrapped her in a blanket, lifted her onto a gurney, and strapped her down. They carried the gurney down two flights of stairs from our apartment to the street. I watched from the second-floor window as they loaded her into the ambulance. Dad stepped into the ambulance, and the doors closed. Flashing lights came on as the ambulance quietly pulled away from the curb and disappeared around a corner.

That morning launched my family on an Accidental Safari that lasted twenty years. My father knew as little about long-term care as he knew about an African Safari, and he proved to be a slow learner. I also knew nothing about Africa or long-term care. I knew little about anything. I was twelve years old.

After many months in the hospital, my mother came home. Her hospitalization was before passage of the 1965 Medicare Amendment to the Social Security Act and before nursing homes. It was also before hospitals provided discharge planning, care plans, and physical rehabilitation. There was only the Visiting Nurse Service of New York. A kind lady came five mornings a week to help us get mother out of bed. After two months, we were on our own.

My mother came home from the hospital to our second-floor apartment in a wheelchair. There were 21 steps from the ground floor to our flat. She had to be pushed or pulled up those 21 steps every time she wanted or needed to go out. She lived in that apartment for the next 15 years, until she moved to a nursing home. To my knowledge, my family never considered moving to a ground-floor apartment. An experienced Safari guide might have suggested it, but we were completely out of our league and on our own.

The mountain of steps into and out of the apartment represented my family's perception of mother's condition. At the time, we did not recognize the fact that there were things we could have and should have done to improve our situation. We did not understand all the pieces of the puzzle, nor did we see how they could fit together. Over time, we learned some basic information about care, but we were totally unaware of a great deal of information that would have been helpful. We did not know what we did not know. And, sadly, much of it we really needed to know.

Today, treatments and therapies are begun in the hospital and continue in a rehabilitation facility. Hospital discharge protocols identify the rehabilitation goals, transitional housing options, and other care resources available to discharged patients. Choices must be made about medications, therapy, feeding tubes and other medical equipment, and whether discharge will be to home or to a rehabilitation facility and, if so, which one. Arrangements must be made concerning paying for care; cashing out retirement funds; applying for financial aid; and obtaining veteran's benefits, powers of attorney, and directives to physicians, among other issues. The list of issues, choices, and decisions may seem endless—and are endless. As each issue arises, an array of available options must be considered.

Many people who suddenly find themselves in this unfamiliar territory, with life on the line, are fearful of making a wrong choice. They are thrust into a jungle where everyone speaks a foreign language, and unseen dangers lurk everywhere. Fear comes because they do not know what lies around the corner or over the next hill. They do not know what to do. What are the options? What happens if a wrong choice is made? People may even experience a paralyzing fear that disaster will strike if they make a bad decision. What if they discover later that a better option was available, but they missed it because they did not know about it?

It is difficult to make decisions in this situation because so much knowledge and information is required to make the best decision. Unfortunately, time doesn't wait, and decisions can't either. Decisions must be made. You cannot stand indefinitely on the plains of the Serengeti, gathering information and contemplating the things you know while also fretting about the things you may not know. Your circumstances require immediate action! So what do most people do in this situation? They take the path of least resistance; the path most traveled. Who can blame them? Numb from shock and exhausted by the emotional and physical effort required to keep breathing and keep moving, the path of least resistance is often the easiest choice. Unfortunately, the path most traveled is often the game trail built by the largest predators.

2

A STRUGGLE FOR SURVIVAL

The Serengeti is a geographical region in Africa that spans 12,000 square miles from northern Tanzania to southwestern Kenya. Due to the tremendous variety of animal life, the Serengeti is a popular tourist destination, with Safaris operated by private businesses and government agencies.

Although wildly beautiful, the Serengeti is perilous. Game is plentiful and predators thrive: lions, cheetahs, wild dogs, hippopotami, mosquitoes, and even tiny tsetse flies. Awareness of the way of the jungle is a must for survival. Death can come from exposure, hunger, thirst, exhaustion, and predators, both animal and human.

IDENTIFYING THE PREDATORS

Is the world in which we live any different? Surrounded as we are by the comforts of America, we do not generally think of life as a daily struggle for survival. We don't need to protect ourselves from lions and tsetse flies. We think only about what's for dinner and getting the car fixed. As we age, however, various threats can sneak up on us and cause us to embark upon an Accidental Safari.

What are those most common risks that can drop someone into an Accidental Safari? The leading causes of hospitalization and death among the elderly can be grouped into three categories: accidents, deterioration of the body, and disorders of the mind. All of them can be perilous.

ACCIDENTS

For the elderly, hospitalization and death due to accidents are generally the result of a combination of events, some of which are truly accidental. According to the American Academy of Family Physicians (AAFP), trauma is the fifth leading cause of death among persons over 65 years of age. Generally, falls are responsible for 70 percent of accidental deaths among people over age 75, but trauma can also be due to traffic accidents and other mishaps. The potential for trauma increases with age for several reasons. Seniors take medications that can affect mobility. Seniors also experience a decrease in balance, body strength, and reaction time and may have cognitive impairments, all of which increase the risk of falls and the degree of injury from them. The elderly, who represent 12 percent of the U.S. population, account for 75 percent of accidental deaths from falls.[1]

Additionally, the number of falls increases progressively with age for both sexes and all racial and ethnic groups. In 2012–2013, the death rate from falls among adults aged 85 and over (226.1 per 100,000) was nearly four times higher than among people aged 75–84 (59.0 per 100,000) and sixteen times higher than among people aged 65–74 (14.1 per 100,000).[2]

"Older adults make up 12% of the U.S. population but account for 18% of all suicide deaths…." Further, elder suicide may be under-reported by 40% or more. Not counted are the "silent suicides," like deaths from overdoses, self-starvation, or dehydration and "accidents…."[3]

It is often impossible to know whether an elderly person who may be suffering from dementia, macular degeneration, and depression, and who is taking a dozen pills a day, has over-dosed accidentally or intentionally.

If the result of a fall is not death, survivors must deal with both healing and recovery, which often result in the need for long-term care.

TWO FALLS, TWO OUTCOMES

John was a commercial airline pilot. He was looking forward to his last two years of employment before mandatory retirement. He anticipated that those two years would yield his highest earnings.

One afternoon, John was putting up Christmas lights at home. It was only a five-foot ladder, what could possibly happen?

When the ladder tipped and John broke both wrists, his wife drove him to the emergency room. By the time John's wrists would heal and he was rehabilitated and recertified to fly, it would be just a few short months before retirement. The airline's physician determined that John should retire immediately.

John's life changed on a dime, but he was lucky. His life journey was interrupted, not derailed.

Eunice was not as fortunate. Her son had come for a visit with his family, including two adult kids and two great-grandchildren. Despite the noise, lunch was an enjoyable affair. The family helped Eunice clean up and left at a reasonable hour. Shortly after they left, however, Eunice decided to return the large salad bowl to its place on a high shelf. She was standing on the stepstool when she fell.

Her son found her two days later, when she hadn't re-sponded to his texts or phone calls. She was alive, but still lying where she had fallen. Her hip and nose were fractured. In a moment, Eunice went from competency to catastrophe. The trauma led to a complete mental and physical collapse. She was lucky to be alive, but was disoriented. Eventually, Eunice was able to walk again, but the fog in her brain never really cleared. She was never again able to return to her home or live on her own. She was moved into an assisted living center near her son.

DETERIORATION OF THE BODY

As with the Trojan Horse in Greek mythology, where warriors hidden inside the horse emerged to attack the city, predators can sometimes attack us from within, without warning, and our Accidental Safari begins. The common predators of body deterioration include heart disease, cancer, stroke, COPD, and scleroderma. These progressive diseases attack us from inside, destroying our body's ability to function as it was designed. Ironically, even after the illness has been identified, the body is often unable to raise a defense to defeat the invading force.

Heart Disease includes heart attacks, angina, and coronary heart disease. It is the leading cause of death among Americans in general and the elderly in particular. Being overweight, having high cholesterol, high blood pressure, or diabetes will increase the chances of heart disease. Symptoms of heart disease can include chest pains and palpitations but, in many cases, there are no symptoms at all.

Cancer diagnoses are ten times greater among people over age 65. In addition to age as a factor, certain chemicals, exposure to radiation, viral infections, and family history can contribute to cancer risk. It is important to understand the risk factors to determine if cancer screening or other early intervention measures might help you.

Stroke is the fourth leading cause of death in the United States. The good news is that the mortality rate from stroke in the United States has decreased over the last several years, and stroke survivors are often able to make a full recovery.

Symptoms of stroke occur suddenly and may include hiccups, nausea, weakness, chest pain, and shortness of breath.

COPD, or chronic obstructive pulmonary disease, is an inflammatory lung disease that generally appears late in life. COPD affects about ten percent of the general population and fifty percent of smokers. Symptoms include coughing, wheezing, and shortness of breath. Many patients ignore these symptoms, which can make diagnosis and treatment more difficult.

Scleroderma is a chronic disease that involves the tightening of one's skin and its connective tissue. There is no cure, but symptoms can be improved with proper treatment. Scleroderma affects the skin, fingers, toes, and internal organs. Complications from the disease can impact almost any part of the body. Fortunately, medication, therapy, and surgery can play a part in helping to relieve scleroderma.

Disorders of the Brain

Our brains can also betray us. Innumerable bodily functions we take entirely for granted are managed by our brain every minute of every day. If our brain takes an unexpected vacation, the result can be an Accidental Safari. A few missed electrical impulses from the brain to the heart can result in sudden cardiac arrest. Brain disorders have several causes that may be either organic and/or external. The result may be a devastating slide in the brain's ability to automatically direct our body to do what needs to be done. As a result, more mental effort must be applied to direct the simplest activities of daily living.

Predatory diseases connected to deterioration of the brain as we age include dementia, Amyotrophic Lateral Sclerosis (ALS), multiple sclerosis, and Parkinson's disease, among others.

Amyotrophic Lateral Sclerosis (ALS) is a progressive disease with a gradual onset that breaks down nerve cells, leading to muscle weakness. There is no cure for the disease, but medication and therapy can help to reduce the accompanying pain and discomfort. This disease affects only motor neurons, so the five senses are left intact. About 6,000 Americans suffer from ALS at any given time, and diagnosis is typically between the ages of 40 and 70.

Multiple Sclerosis (MS) is a progressive disease in which the myelin sheath surrounding the nerves is gradually destroyed by the body's immune system. MS is generally diagnosed between the ages of 20 and 50. The mental and physical symptoms of MS frequently overlap with other symptoms of aging such as fatigue, muscle weakness, imbalance, and cognitive and memory impairment. While MS isn't a terminal illness, and the average lifespan of someone with MS is about 76 years, a diagnosis may lead to many years of care.

Parkinson's Disease (PD) is a progressive, chronic disease that affects the central nervous system. Many of the symptoms of PD are the result of a loss of dopamine-producing neurons in the brain. One of the early signs of PD is a slight tremor in one hand. Generally the disease presents on one side of the body first. That side will remain the most affected, even as the symptoms have spread to the other side.

Dementia tends to affect people beginning at age 65, but an early onset of the disorder can affect people as young as age 30.

One of the most common types of dementia is Alzheimer's disease. Approximately three million people in the United States are diagnosed with a form of dementia each year. Symptoms can vary greatly but tend to center around impaired memory and communication, lack of focus, and reduced reasoning/judgment. Although there is presently no cure for dementia or Alzheimer's, research is ongoing to find therapies and medications to slow or stop their progress. Additionally, medications have been found that can relieve some of the symptoms.

ALZHEIMER'S: A LONELY JOURNEY

Charlie and Mary's life journey together was diverted by an Accidental Safari. After retirement, the couple moved into a retirement community in the Pacific Northwest. They were both fun loving and outgoing. Charlie was a social animal and had never met a stranger. He loved people, and he never forgot a name. To fill her free time, Mary became a realtor.

Before retirement, Charlie had been a high school shop teacher. He loved to tinker and fix things and was meticulous in his work. Mary liked to say that the only thing Charlie couldn't fix was "the crack of dawn and a broken heart." He'd earned his students' respect because they knew he cared about them. If a student submitted a poorly crafted project, Charlie knew how to challenge the student to do better the next time.

He shared his wisdom about life and would often quote author and motivational speaker Zig Ziglar, who said, "Doing your best is more important than being the best."

When Charlie and Mary purchased a home on the golf course, Charlie bought the golf cart along with the house. He enjoyed playing golf in the light northwest rain and played often after the move. Meanwhile, Mary was learning the ropes of real estate in their new town. Her business seemed to go well from the start. Mary's kind manner and professionalism had seemed to open a spigot in town, and new business was flowing in. Whenever something needed to be repaired at one of Mary's listings, she would call on Charlie. Although Charlie enjoyed coming to the rescue, it was really beginning to cut into his golf game, especially when the new owners would call him back to do additional improvements. Each project seemed to take more and more time and effort to complete, and Charlie played golf less and less often.

As time passed, an incident occurred that caught Mary by surprise. Charlie was supposed to meet her at a client's home to replace a small sliding window in an outside door. Charlie had left for the hardware store, but was late arriving back at the client's home. Mary kept busy, but she recognized how uncharacteristically late he was. She called him several times. He finally picked up on her fifth call.

"What's the matter?" he asked.

"What's the matter with you? Where are you? Why did you hang up?"

There was silence on the phone. "Charlie, are you there? Charlie?"

"Yes, yes, I'm here . . . I'm kind of lost."

Charlie was only a few blocks away, but he had made a wrong turn into a cul-de-sac, where he became confused and immobilized. When his phone rang, it had brought him back, but then he'd pressed a wrong button and accidentally hung up. Charlie wanted to brush it off. He was confused about what had happened and didn't want to worry Mary, but Mary had noticed.

A similar occurrence took place a few days later when Charlie returned to install the replacement window. Mary was signing some papers with the homeowner. She expected Charlie to finish before she did, but when all of her business, including the small talk, was concluded, Charlie had still not appeared. Mary went to find him. As she rounded a corner she found Charlie standing motionless. Something stopped her from speaking. She simply watched him as he stood still for a long time. She followed Charlie's gaze to the floor and saw the old window and the new window laying next to each other. She stepped up to him and quietly asked him, "How's it going, dear? Can I give you a hand? What do you need?"

"I got it" he said and picked up the small window and moved toward the door. As he fit the replacement window into the door, he asked her to hand him the drill. They had to stop briefly to look for a package of screws that had come with the window and were ultimately found in Charlie's pocket. Charlie fit the window into the door and asked Mary to hand him the drill again. Mary could see that the new window was upside down.

And so began Charlie and Mary's Accidental Safari into the dark jungle of Alzheimer's disease. Charlie presented very well. At first, even Mary couldn't tell if she was speaking to the old Charlie or if he was simply replaying familiar conversations that had worn a groove in his brain. But the brain pathways were getting increasingly blocked, and the flow of clever quips, kindness, and self-sufficiency were disappearing into a cul-de-sac inside Charlie's head. Charlie and Mary found themselves taking a journey together, yet alone.

The problem with time is that we think we have it. From the moment we are born, each one of us is on an inescapable journey into the future—one that may involve an Accidental Safari that leads to long-term care. Remember, as the *Lion King* said, life is a circle, from birth to death. Therefore, it is important for us to view our need for care at the end of our lives as an expected part of the journey, rather than as an unexpected penalty called in the final minutes of the game. As we were celebrated at birth with tender care and attention, so we should celebrate life at full circle, when our care needs are once again high. *We all must take this life-and-death journey.*

While the disorders we have discussed here are the most common, the above list is not exhaustive. A sudden fall or an accident is akin to an unexpected attack from a violent predator on Safari; a progressive disease or disorder of the body or the brain is like the malaria-carrying mosquito in the camp. The victim may be miles down the road, and the predatory mosquito long forgotten, before the thought occurs, "Could this be malaria?"

3

THE ROAD MOST TAKEN

The emergency room is often the first stop on the Accidental Safari. An accidental fall may be your ticket there. A heart attack, stroke, dehydration, or even a urinary tract infection, may also take you there. Eventually, even slow-moving illnesses such as Parkinson's, ALS, and Alzheimer's will lead you there.

The emergency room may be only the first stop on the Accidental Safari, but it is vital that you understand the "rules of the road" from the very beginning.

FIRST STOP: THE EMERGENCY ROOM

On August 7, 2016, a small article appeared in *The New York Times*. Although it appeared innocuous at first glance, upon closer inspection it contained a bombshell of information. It read:

New Medicare Law to Notify

WASHINGTON — In November, after a bad fall, 85-year-old Elizabeth Cannon was taken to a hospital outside Philadelphia for six and a half days of "observation," followed by nearly five months at a nearby nursing home for rehabilitation and skilled nursing care. The cost: more than $40,000.

The hospital insisted that Ms. Cannon had never been formally admitted as an inpatient, so under federal rules, Medicare would not pay for her nursing home stay. The money would have to come from her pocket.

(https://www.nytimes.com/2016/08/07/us/politics/new-medicare-law-to-notify-patients-of-loophole-in-nursing-home-coverage.html)[4]

If you are over the age of 65 or have been receiving Social Security Disability benefits for two years or more, you qualify for Medicare. Medicare is government health insurance for the disabled and for those over 65 years of age. Although many people consider Medicare to be a "healthcare program," the fact is that Medicare primarily covers "medical care." It is critical to know the distinction between these two terms. "Medical care" and "health care" are not interchangeable when it comes to Medicare. In fact, when a health problem ceases to be a "medical" issue and becomes a "care" issue, Medicare coverage will come to an end.

In the emergency room, medical personnel will evaluate your condition to determine if there is a medical reason for you to stay in the hospital. If you are there because something hurts, you feel dizzy, or you simply feel terrible, the emergency room physician will run a battery of tests. They may perform an EKG, a blood test, blood pressure test, or x-ray. They may run all these tests and more. The tests could, and usually do, take hours. Once all the test results are in, the doctor will decide whether to send you home or admit you to the hospital. If no apparent medical reason can be found to keep you, you will be sent home. If the test results indicate a serious problem, you will be admitted to the hospital for "treatment." However, if medical personnel agree that something is going on, but they cannot determine what it is from the test results, they may put you in a hospital room "under observation."

If you know that something is "not right," but they find no reason to keep you in the hospital and choose to send you home, you should ask—even demand—that you be allowed to stay at the hospital. If the staff refuses to admit you and declares that they are finished treating you, you can refuse to leave. I do not recommend that course of action. If they cannot or will not treat you, go directly and immediately to another hospital or urgent care facility. I have heard many stories from clients who were turned out of the hospital even though they (the clients) were certain that they needed help and could not adequately care for themselves. A hospital cannot refuse to examine you (and treat you), but once you have been examined (and treated), they can decide whether or not there is a medical reason to keep you.

A heart attack will definitely keep you in the hospital. A stroke will likely keep you in the hospital, if there are obvious symptoms or if a brain scan shows damage. However, if the emergency room physician decides there is no medical reason to keep you in the hospital, you will be released.

To recap, you can be given a hospital room in one of two ways. You will either be "admitted" to the hospital as a patient, or you will be placed in the hospital room "under observation." If there is a clear medical reason for you to stay, and you are on Medicare, you will be "admitted" as a patient. But, if the tests are inconclusive and merely suggest that there *might* be something going on medically, you may be given the room "under observation." It is surprising to many people to learn that you can be placed in a hospital room for "observation" and not technically be a patient of the hospital!

PRIVATE PAY VS. MEDICARE

In other words, the way that your hospital stay is classified when you move from the emergency room to the hospital room is of critical importance. If you happen to be Elizabeth Cannon (in *The New York Times* article above) and you have been given a hospital room "for observation," the Accidental Safari will cost you dearly.

The New York Times article describes the "Notice Act" signed into law on August 6, 2015. The Act requires hospitals to present you with a notice within 36 hours of being placed in a hospital room under "observation." You are required to sign the notice. If you refuse to sign the notice, it will be signed for you.

At this point it becomes extremely important that you have an advocate to join you on the Safari. This may be a spouse, a child, or other concerned individual who will be with you on this phase of the journey. When you are moved from the emergency room, you (or your advocate) should confirm that you are being admitted as a "patient" and not being moved to a room "under observation." Check the designated box on the admitting document as confirmation. If you discover that you are being "observed," it is important to ask someone in authority two questions immediately: "Why haven't I been admitted as a patient?" and "What will it take to get me admitted as a patient?" Don't hesitate to ask to be re-classified. Hospital personnel know how the system works. I have had more than one medical professional suggest to me that a patient may want to have an accidental "fall" on the way to the bathroom to ensure that he or she gets admitted as a "patient." Don't be afraid to make a fuss, you have a right to the information!

It is very important to be "admitted" to the hospital as a patient rather than placed "under observation" because if you are on Medicare and spend three (3) full days as a patient in the hospital before being transferred to a rehabilitation facility, Medicare will pay 100% of the cost of rehabilitation for the first 20 days; costs that can exceed $300.00 per day. The cost of those 20 days can exceed $10,000 between the expenses of room and board, nursing care, occupational therapy, physical therapy, and speech therapy.

After the first 20 days, Medicare will pay all but the first (approximately) $157.00 per day for the next 80 days. While Medicare is paying the "back end" expenses (costs in excess of $157.00 per day), most seniors have supplemental health insurance that will cover the "front end" expenses (the first $157.00 in expenses per day) of those 80 days. Not all supplemental insurance plans pay the front end, so check your supplemental insurance plan to be certain that it will cover the first $157.00 if Medicare is covering the rest.

Unfortunately, the Notice Act passed by Congress does not address this injustice, it just acknowledges it. In 2016, *The New York Times* article continued with this explanation:

> Hospitals have found themselves in a squeeze. They increased their use of "observation status" in response to close scrutiny of their billing practices by Medicare auditors—private companies hired by the government to review claims. In many cases, these companies challenged decisions by doctors to admit patients to a hospital, saying the services should have been provided on an outpatient basis. The auditors then tried to recover what they described as improper payments. Doctors and hospitals said the auditors were like bounty hunters because they were allowed to keep a percentage of the funds they recovered.

Under the Act, hospitals are simply required to inform patients that Medicare will not pay, at a time when there is little or nothing a patient can do. The moral of the story is that you need to ensure that if at all possible you, or your loved one, is "admitted" as a patient.

The Accidental Safari has hardly left base camp, and this one little bend in the road could end up costing you tens of thousands of dollars for those initial 100 days of care. Inexperienced travelers need to stay close to the guide. If you do not have a guide, get one. You can't afford to make mistakes on an Accidental Safari, if you hope to survive.

A RIDE ON THE MEDICARE-GO-ROUND

Allen and Beverly were inseparable. He had recently retired as the Information Technology Manager for a credit union. Together, they started a small business, offering web page design to small companies. Beverly handled the marketing, and Allen created websites. They had never been diligent savers, so they needed the extra income from this new business venture to supplement their Social Security and retirement income.

Beverly was a go-getter. Over the next eight years, they built a steady business. Suddenly and unexpectedly, however, Allen began to experience frequent and severe nausea in the mornings. He would vomit violently. He discovered that if he ate early in the day and ate very little in the evening, his mornings were slightly more tolerable. He experienced "dry heaves," but less actual vomiting.

Allen and Beverly's Accidental Safari had begun, though they didn't know it. The journey started with a doctor's appointment. That appointment was followed by referrals to numerous specialists and included a visit to a local teaching hospital. None of Allen's test results pointed to an identifiable illness. He was given no diagnosis, no prescriptions, no treatment, and no relief. Allen endured his symptoms for two miserable years.

Allen was a big man and initially managed to maintain his weight. He was a man's man who always had a project going around the house. Now, however, it was all he could do to mow the small lawn in the back yard. His activity level dropped precipitously, and so did the business. Allen grew more and more frail. His sense of humor dried up. He was weary of the daily battle with an unknown enemy. He felt lousy all the time.

I ran into Allen one day outside my office. I couldn't help noticing his weak handshake. In fact, his hand felt soft, like a child's hand. I looked down and observed that his hand looked like it had been doing very little.

Soon after our meeting, while Allen was at home unloading the car, he found that he was having trouble holding onto the groceries. He dropped several items. Thinking he was just tired, he went to lie down in the house. He felt no better after his rest, so Beverly drove him to the emergency room. The Accidental Safari began to pick up steam as they entered the emergency room.

Allen could move all of his working parts, but he felt a little disoriented and weak on his left side. He was placed in a hospital room "under observation" and to run some tests.

The doctors suspected that he had suffered a transient ischemic attack (TIA), often called a mini-stroke. TIAs and strokes have the same cause. The only way to tell the difference between a TIA and a stroke is by looking at an image of the brain through either a CT or an MRI scan. Proper diagnosis is important because the effects of a TIA are temporary and usually do not cause permanent damage to brain tissue. Strokes will result in permanent damage to brain tissue. If you have experienced a TIA, you are at high risk of experiencing a full stroke. One (1) in three (3) people who have a TIA will have a stroke at some point, and early treatment is absolutely essential for recovery. (http://www.healthline.com/health/stroke/signs-symptoms-tia-mini-stroke#Whatisaministroke?1)[5]

Allen spent his first night in the hospital under observation. The next morning, an aide came to take him for tests. She asked him to transfer into a wheelchair. As he was rising from the bed, he unexpectedly collapsed to the floor, severely injuring his right shoulder and hip. His status changed from "under observation" to "patient" in the blink of an eye.

After x-rays, scans, blood tests, stomach tests, and a myriad of other tests, it was determined that Allen had suffered a stroke that had caused his fall. The fall bruised, but didn't break, his right shoulder and hip. The doctor said the tests also suggested that Allen had a condition known as a "lazy" stomach. He was prescribed a medication that minimized the nausea and stopped the vomiting: a medication that he had desperately needed for two years!

Allen's follow-up testing, analysis, review, consulta-tion, and agreement as to a future course of action took five days, (which met the three-day hospital stay requirement) after which Allen was moved to a reha-bilitation facility, under Medicare.

NO SHORT CUTS ON THE ROAD TO REHABILITATION

The path from the hospital leads through diagnosis to treatment. A patient will generally remain in the hospital for treatment and additional tests. Often, then rehabilitation will begin. The main goal of rehabilitation is to restore health and function, but sometimes there is little hope for improvement. Although some hospitals provide rehabilitation services, the vast majority of hospitals send patients (or the person under "observation") to a rehabilitation facility or a skilled nursing facility. Rehabilitation can also take place at home.

If rehabilitation is ordered, the patient's advocate will work with the hospital discharge planner to take the following actions:

Choose a rehabilitation facility. The goal is to choose a facility that can provide the kind of treatment and programs the patient needs. The primary purpose of this phase of care is to get the patient back to his/her former level of mobility and quality of life, while addressing the patient's underlying medi-cal issues.

Whether you have little opinion about rehabilitation facili-ties or have a strong preference for a particular one, an impor-tant consideration is room availability. It is not uncommon for good facilities to have a waiting list, which may mean that a patient has to move temporarily to a less-desirable facility until space becomes available.

Some supplemental insurance companies have preferences and may require their policy holders to use a particular facility. The hospital discharge planner or insurance company may make it appear that the contracted facility is the best place, or even the only place, for the patient. They may suggest that nothing else is available, while your request for a particular facility is ignored. The truth is there is a lot of money on the table during this stage of the journey. During the rehabilitative period, the fees paid by Medicare and supplemental insurance companies to the rehabilitation facility are higher than the fees Medicaid will pay a facility. There may also be a contract between your supplemental insurance carrier and a particular facility that influences the choice of facilities.

The location of the facility should have a high priority in the selection. It is best to choose a facility as close to the patient's advocate as possible. The advocate is not merely a cheerleader for the patient. He or she is a lifeline. At this stage of the process, the advocate must be on hand regularly to monitor and take notes on the patient's daily progress and ensure that his/her needs are being fully met. The advocate must carefully document any and all physical improvement as well as any observed obstacles to improvement. The advocate needs to attend all care meetings at the facility and be ready to discuss his/her observations and make appeals and demands for further services. The patient, and even the advocate, can feel overwhelmed at this stage and may not be aware of the best questions to ask or be prepared to make demands for needed services. The assistance of an independent geriatric care manager could be extremely helpful at this stage.

A geriatric care manager is typically an independent registered nurse or social worker who is not connected to the facility in any capacity. He/she is able to assess the situation and determine if the care being provided is meeting the patient's needs. A geriatric care manager can provide additional weight if your voice is not being adequately heard. He/she will serve as a guide to teach you what you need to know to survive this part of the journey.

Break camp and move on. Whether you feel that the hospital has done a great job in identifying and addressing the patient's issues, or you cannot wait to leave the hospital, moving to a rehabilitation facility is entering a new phase of the Accidental Safari. And change is always stressful because of the unknowns involved.

The first order of business in the rehabilitation facility will be to review the directives and medications prescribed by the hospital, perform an assessment, and create a personal care plan. A physical therapist, an occupational therapist, a speech therapist, a social worker and, in many cases, a psychologist, will meet with the patient and the advocate.

The physical therapist's (PT's) job is to get the patient moving again. PTs help the patient learn to walk again, with or without a cane or a walker, or learn to use a wheelchair. They instruct patients on transferring themselves from a bed to a chair or toilet. The goal is physical independence for the patient, to the extent possible.

The occupational therapist's (OT's) job is to help the patient re-learn the tasks of self-care such as brushing teeth, putting on shoes, getting dressed, and using a cell phone. It can be very frustrating to the patient to have to retrain the body to do the simple tasks that we all take for granted. Patience and encouragement from the advocate and others is necessary at this time. As with physical therapy, the goal of occupational therapy is patient independence.

The speech therapist's (ST's) job is to help the patient regain lost communication skills. In addition to speech therapy, the therapist helps with reading, writing, and swallowing. Difficulty in swallowing can be a life-threatening condition. As with the other therapies, the goal of speech therapy is independence for the patient.

Rehabilitation is a critical stage of the journey. It is hard work, and patients are expected to participate in the process as fully as they are able. In the Safari analogy, it is not equivalent to sipping a frozen daiquiri while observing the African savannah from the comfort of an air-conditioned tour bus. Rehabilitation is like carrying a heavy backpack and canteen, trudging up and down hills in scorching heat, while studying a map and keeping a watchful eye out for predators.

Rehabilitation therapy is designed to take weeks, not months; that is why Medicare participates in the costs of rehabilitation for only 100 days. The reality is that therapy can be extremely challenging for the patient. If the patient has just been released from the hospital, he/she may feel fragile and not completely "right." In therapy sessions, patients are challenged to perform numerous tasks they may feel incapable of doing or fearful of attempting. Because the ultimate goal of therapy is independence for the patient, therapy must be done "with" the patient and cannot be done "for" the patient. Rehabilitation is not a spectator sport.

A major problem with rehabilitation is motivation. People on an Accidental Safari are sick, and they are tired. They may still be in shock from the sudden and violent abduction from their "real" life and aren't yet fully aware that they have been forcibly thrust into this unplanned adventure. They certainly do not want to be on this adventure. Therefore, it can be expected that they will have some degree of emotional difficulty buying into the program.

Additionally, they may be ill-equipped for rehabilitation because they have a progressive illness and simply lack the physical strength or will power to make the necessary effort to progress and return to their former life. In such an instance, many simply give up. And for some who are failing in mind and/or body, no amount of encouragement or effort can change the inevitable outcome.

There are also the adventurers, the plodders, and the workers. These people are the ones who will do anything and everything in their power to survive the Accidental Safari. They are not ready for their life journey to end. They make forward progress through sheer determination and through their own power, with or without the aid of a walker or a wheelchair. Clyde was one such person.

A WILL TO SURVIVE

Clyde had a stroke when he was 80 years of age. The stroke completely paralyzed his right side. He told me that shortly after the stroke his doctor explained the possible long-term consequences and identified the activities that Clyde would likely be able to do again, as well as the things he would probably not be able to do.

With a sparkle in his eye, Clyde said to me, "So, I asked the doctor..." (Clyde began to slur his speech dramatically as he told me the story) "Sooo, Docta, ah luv da byolin (violin). Will ah eva be able to play da byolin?"

The doctor, trying his best to be encouraging, said, "Well, Mr. Smith, if you work very hard, I am sure you will be able to play the violin again."

To this Clyde responded, "Dat's goood, Docta, because I could neva play da byolin befo."

Clyde was an avid fisherman. After the stroke, he was determined to regain the skills he'd lost. Initially, he would sit, until he could eventually stand, at one end of the long hall in the nursing home, with his fishing rod in hand. He would practice casting his line into a bucket at the end of the hall. He cast his line over and over and over again, until he had regained full use of his limbs.

Clyde refused to stay on the Accidental Safari. He worked diligently to recover from the stroke and return to his old life. Today, more than ten years later, Clyde enjoys his life much as he had before the stroke. Clyde is one of those people who refused to give up.

Advocates should record the patient's capabilities at the time he/she enters the rehabilitation facility. Following the initial assessment by the staff, usually within the first few days, a care conference will be held. In attendance will be the physical therapist, the occupational therapist, the speech therapist, the nurse, the social worker, the patient, and the patient's advocate.

During the conference, an individual care plan is laid out, which details the course of therapy to be followed for the next days and weeks. Goals and expectations are specifically detailed. The medical team should plainly state what they believe to be the restorative potential of the therapy for the client. If a patient or advocate has any questions, comments, or concerns, this is the ideal time to spell them out. Don't hesitate to voice your expectations, needs, and disappointments about anything— from the food, to the care plan, to the attitudes of the staff. If the response is unacceptable, speak directly to the facility's head administrator. Identify the problems you have had or can see on the horizon.

If the staff is not responsive, complain to the facility director and/or file a formal complaint with the state. The last resort is move to a different facility, if your supplemental insurance carrier will allow it. The facility wants what they think is best. Make sure the decision on what is best is one shared by all parties.

After the initial care conference, the patient may feel as though he/she has awakened from a nightmare and landed in "boot camp." An intensive regimen of therapies begins. The advocate should observe and record the process, carefully noting any progress made by the patient. The level of progress will, hopefully, be evident but, if not, the advocate should note any improvement, however slight. If the patient could not hold a spoon when he/she entered the facility, but can now eat unassisted, that fact should be documented. If he/she can stand in place, turn toward the wheelchair, or take two steps more than was possible previously, it should be noted.

This progress record will become extremely important in the days to come. After a few days or weeks of rehabilitation, another meeting with the medical team will be scheduled. This second care meeting will review the patient's progress and propose a path forward. However, if the professionals think the patient has stopped moving toward his/her restorative potential, and the likelihood of further improvement has leveled off, the purpose of the meeting will be to explain that the patient has reached a plateau.

The therapist must be able to document progress in order to continue the patient's Medicare eligibility. The therapist walks a fine line between doing too much and pushing the patient too hard and just covering the required bases so that no one can point a finger and suggest that they dropped the ball. To illustrate, let's pick up on our previous story about Allen and Beverly's Ride on the Medicare-Go-Round.

THE MEDICARE-GO-ROUND, PART II

Allen was relieved to be out of the hospital but was unhappy that he wasn't at home. He wasn't happy in the rehabilitation center, despite its high ratings. Beverly was armed and ready to battle for her husband, but from his first days at the facility, he did not fare well. The speech therapist determined that the risk of aspiration was high, so she placed him on a liquid diet including "thick water." As a result, Allen found everything on the menu extremely uninviting. Consequently, he consumed less than 500 calories per day and grew steadily weaker. Beverly was advised that Allen should suck on ice chips to stay hydrated, but whenever she visited, the ice cup was either not on the bedside table within reach, or the ice had melted.

Allen was not consuming enough calories to survive. The staff thought that if they had him get out of bed for dinner, it might stimulate his appetite. Allen, however, was not excited about the ordeal of getting up, and it was painful for him to sit a long time. He was the only diner seated at a table for four. Beverly was next to him urging him to eat. Across from them sat a young woman whose assignment was to take note of everything he consumed.

As the cover was lifted off his dinner plate, Allen saw mashed potatoes, whipped carrots, and pureed meat of unknown origin. He dipped the corner of his fork into the potatoes and took a tiny taste.

Allen was done. He sat there for another ten minutes looking at the tray and listening to Beverly try to convince him that the food was fit for human consumption. He looked at the young woman and announced "I hurt; I want to go to bed."

No one moved. Allen said it again, a lot louder the second time and with tone. "I HURT, AND I WANT TO GO TO BED."

Beverly moved behind Allen while the calorie counter said, "I will let them know."

Beverly pushed Allen back to his room, where they waited for 10 minutes for someone to help put Allen to bed. As she realized that his pain was becoming intolerable, Beverly cornered an aide and told him that Allen needed to be put to bed immediately. The aide's response was, "We will get right to it."

Another 10 minutes passed. Beverly tracked down the aide and demanded that Allen be put to bed immediately. She was told, "He needs to be up for thirty minutes after dinner." With great control, Beverly told the aide that Allen had had no dinner. He responded, "I will check on that and be right back."

Unfortunately, this is typical of a system that employs a "check the box" protocol. The calorie counter may have told the nurse on duty that Allen was finished with dinner and wanted to go to bed. She may have told them that he had eaten only a single bite for dinner. But no one was going to break the rule that requires a thirty-minute wait period between dinner and being put to bed— pain be damned. The staff was trained to check all the boxes and go by the book, but was not trained to put a patient's needs first. They lacked the understanding and personal courage to address the needs of the patient.

A "check the box" system directs the manner in which Medicare determines continued eligibility for rehabilitation services. If too few boxes are checked and it is determined that a plateau has been reached, the rules state that Medicare payments must cease.

HITTING A PLATEAU: LOOK AROUND

When you reach a plateau on the Accidental Safari, the landscape will look unchanging and desolate, as far as the eye can see. The good news, however, is that when you can see a great distance, you can also see what's coming toward you. It's harder to be surprised and easier to determine which direction to go. Do not lose heart!

At this point, the records kept by the patient and/or advocate will play an essential role. If the staff and therapists agree that the patient has reached a plateau, you can expect to hear it at the next care meeting. The advocate's job will be to identify the areas where progress has been made but was understated or overlooked by the care team or provide a reasonable explanation for the lack of progress.

The impact of this relates to Medicare coverage. The rehabilitation facility must be able to show the Medicare auditors that sufficient progress has been made to warrant continued rehabilitation. The job of the advocate is to give the medical team enough additional information about the patient's progress, and/or enough explanation for the lack of progress, that the medical team can check all the boxes necessary to satisfy Medicare that rehabilitation should continue.

If the advocate is unable to convince the medical team that therapy should continue, the patient will receive a notice of Medicare termination. The notice of termination will provide information and instructions about how to appeal the decision. Unfortunately, the time period for filing an appeal is extremely short; just one business day from receipt of the termination notice. On the upside, the appeal process requires only a telephone call.

As the patient's advocate, you can be ready for this action. Atop the plateau, you have seen this termination coming and were not taken by surprise. You have observed and recorded the rehabilitation process and, with your documentation in hand, you are ready to make the phone call.

The goal in making the appeal is to give the Medicare representative enough information to check the right number of boxes, so that Medicare will continue to pay for rehabilitation. It is not unusual for a facility to pull the plug early on therapy to avoid the possibility that a Medicare auditor may accuse them of continuing rehabilitation too long. Medicare pays the facility generously, so there is always a potential for "fraud" in the process. If Medicare determined that a facility continued to provide therapy or other services that a patient didn't need or that wouldn't make any material difference in the patient's outcome, a charge of fraud could be filed by Medicare against the facility.

If you win the appeal, the facility can continue to serve the patient without fear of reprisal from Medicare. This is a win-win outcome, so make the call! Allen and Beverly discovered the significance of the plateau as they continued on their Medicare-Go-Round.

THE MEDICARE-GO-ROUND, PART III

Allen was a big man and, because he was completely immobile, all transfers between the bed and wheelchair were done using a Hoyer lift, a mechanical device that allows a person to be lifted and transferred with a minimum of physical effort. He was taken to therapy every day, where not much happened. Allen's hip and shoulder injury were so painful that he was not able to participate in physical therapy. Allen was getting weaker by the day. The doctor stopped by on the evening of Allen's fourth day in rehabilitation. He agreed that Allen was not taking in enough water or calories to survive. Allen was failing fast.

The physician ordered Allen back to the hospital on the following day for insertion of a nasogastric (nose to stomach) feeding tube. After the procedure, Allen was returned to the rehabilitation facility, where he began to improve. His stomach problems had improved through medication, and he was able to keep food down. Sadly, when the feeding tube was removed, Allen showed little interest in eating and he still could not, or would not, participate in physical therapy.

Another meeting of the medical team was called. Allen and Beverly were present. It was announced that Allen had hit a plateau and would be moved to a nursing home. The medical team knew this meant the end of physical therapy. Allen and Beverly did not understand this fact.

Beverly was given a Notice of Medicare Termination, which offered information about the 24-hour appeal window. Beverly took Allen back to his room, where they reviewed what had happened at the meeting. They discussed the improvements Allen thought he was making and the compelling reasons for his lack of progress in other areas. Allen explained that he could now sit up on the side of the bed and that he could stand. Beverly had not seen him do either of these things. She wondered if he was imagining that he was sitting up independently and standing, even though he wasn't. Could these imagined results be due to the tremendous mental effort he was exerting in an effort to get his body to obey what his mind was demanding? Allen further explained that the pain in his hip and shoulder were the primary reason he could not fully engage in his physical therapy. He pointed out that he was taking in a little solid food and water without assistance. These were the elements of progress Beverly would explain during the Medicare appeal to try to win an extension of Allen's rehabilitation time.

Beverly thought the call went well. She cried but was able to explain everything she had written down. She was told to expect a decision within 48 hours. Allen would not be moved until the appeal was decided.

They received the news two days later that they had won the appeal!

Physical therapy began again. It was a hard week and, unfortunately, no progress was made. This time, after just seven days of the renewed intensive therapy plan, another care meeting was called. At the meeting, another Notice of Termination was issued, with another right to appeal. Beverly appealed again, but the appeal was denied.

A unilateral decision was made by the patient's medical team that, in their opinion, he was not going to improve, so Medicare stopped paying, they stopped rehabilitative therapy, and Allen was moved to nursing care.

THE WASHOUT: NO WAY FORWARD AND NO WAY BACK

Allen and Beverly had reached another pivotal point in the Accidental Safari: a washout. A washout occurs when the solid ground you are traveling on is suddenly gone, and there is no clear path forward or back. It is extremely important to be aware of, and to carefully consider, all the options available at this junction. Critical decisions about housing, care, and costs need to be made, all of which will have lasting and significant implications. Many people are overwhelmed by the stress of having to make these difficult decisions. There is no assurance that all of the available options have been presented. The professional therapists, who were supposed to guide you, are not much help at this stage. They will turn their attention to their current patients, including the one that will now take your room. This is the point at which it may seem that all hope is gone.

The Accidental Safari has reached an impasse. You need independent advice. It is more important than ever that you find a guide to navigate the changing landscape. You do not want someone who has a connection to the rehabilitation facility that you are leaving.

Get a referral from someone you trust to a geriatric care manager, social worker, and/or an elder law attorney. You will need someone who has a reputation for successfully navigating the Safari. Then sit down, catch your breath, and get clarity about the alternative paths ahead. Each path will present unique challenges and require different skills and supplies. The likelihood that you will be able to successfully traverse the path ahead will be influenced by many variables. There is no "one size fits all" Accidental Safari.

On January 24, 2013, the U. S. District Court for the District of Vermont approved a settlement agreement in the case of Jimmo v. Sebelius

In the Jimmo case, the Center for Medicare Advocacy (CMA) argued that the patient, Glenda Jimmo, and many people all over the nation who were similarly situated, had their Medicare benefits (specifically the right to receive therapy) denied, reduced, or terminated because of an unlawful standard that Medicare required improvement by the patient for coverage eligibility. The United States District Court in Vermont ruled that while the Medicare rules do not support a standard of improvement, coverage is not required in a situation where the needs of the patient can be met with unskilled care, even though the lack of therapy results in a long, slow decline in the patient's health and abilities.

(http://www.medicareadvocacy.org/self-help-packet-for-expedited-skilled-nursing-facility-appeals-including-improvement-standard-denials/)6

The Center for Medicare Advocacy (CMA) has a comprehensive website that contains specific, free self-help packets. Each packet provides a step-by-step guide to confront the common pitfalls at the beginning of the Accidental Safari:

- Choosing Between Traditional Medicare and a Medicare Advantage Plan

- Self-Help Packet for Ambulance Appeals

- Self-Help Packet for Outpatient Therapy Denials Including "Improvement Standard" Denials

- Self-Help Packet for Home Health Care Appeals Including "Improvement Standard" Denials

- Self-Help Packet for Hospital Discharge

- Self-Help Packet for Skilled Nursing Facility Appeals Including "Improvement Standard" Denials

- Advocacy Tips: Medicare Administrative Law Judge (ALJ) Hearing Process

(http://www.medicareadvocacy.org/take-action/self-help-packets-for-medicare-appeals/)7

THE MEDICARE-GO-ROUND, PART IV

Now that Medicare-funded rehabilitation was at an end, Allen and Beverly were presented with several options, each of which had positive and negative aspects. The options included the following:

Staying at the rehabilitation facility. Allen would have to pay privately for continued therapy, and the total out-of-pocket costs would exceed $13,000 per month. Allen and Beverly were familiar with the facility, the staff, and the routine. Unfortunately, the relationship with the staff was strained because the staff had expressed no confidence in Allen's ability to improve.

Moving to a nursing home. Allen was still profoundly paralyzed on his left side. In a nursing home, he would receive the level of care his paralysis required (a Hoyer lift was still needed to transfer him from bed to wheelchair). Although physical therapy was available in the nursing home, it would add substantially to his daily cost of care. Allen was discouraged by his lack of progress and was no longer interested in continuing the "torture treatment," as he called it. The cost of room, board, and care, without physical therapy, would be approximately $9,000 per month, by private payment, without help from Medicare or supplemental insurance.

Moving to a less expensive facility that offers fewer services. This move would reduce the out-of-pocket expenses, but Allen's needs for care were at a level beyond what a less-costly facility could provide.

Moving home. This was Allen's first choice. When asked what he wanted, Allen replied, "I want to go home where I can sit in my chair, sleep next to my wife, and pet my dog." This was Beverly's choice as well. Unfortunately, neither Beverly, nor their home, were able to accommodate Allen's physical needs. Allen required a level of care that would be very difficult for Beverly to provide, on her own, at home.

Allen was moved from the rehabilitation facility to a nursing home. Their out-of-pocket cost-of-care was

$290.00 per day. The cost was significantly less than the rehabilitation facility, but the nursing home offered no physical therapy and, therefore, no hope of recovery. Medicare and Allen's supplemental insurance would not pay because the appeal denial had determined that coverage "would not be available in a situation where the beneficiary's care needs can be addressed safely and effectively through the use of unskilled personnel."

Allen seemed more engaged after he arrived at the nursing home. He was talking more and asking questions about breakfast in the morning.

The next morning, the staff got Allen up and brought him to the dining room. He sat at the end of a long table with eight other residents. They were all in wheelchairs. The staff was very friendly and interacted with the residents. It was not the deathly silence that can sometimes fill a room in a nursing home.

The staff went out of their way to make sure that Allen could find something he liked at breakfast. They gave him eggs, bacon, sausage, pancakes, oatmeal, and a donut, along with coffee, water, and orange juice. Allen joked that it was better than a grand slam breakfast at Denny's restaurant.

He began to eat slowly. After seven or eight bites, he put his fork down and waved at the server. He told her he was feeling nauseous. She gave him a bucket and moved him away from the table. That was the end. At that point, Allen made the decision to stop eating and drinking altogether. When he put his fork down, the battle was over. Allen had surrendered.

He told Beverly that he wanted to go home. He said little else. He did not respond to her pleas to eat and drink.

Beverly met with the local hospice team who helped make arrangements for a hospital bed and in-home caregivers to assist with Allen's care. Beverly found a neighbor who would build a ramp to get his wheelchair up the three steps to the front door. Their two daughters came and tenderly administered to them during the last week of Allen's life. All three were at his bedside when he died. He had been at home for less than two weeks.

In July, 2003, a New England Journal of Medicine article stated that "Nurses reported that patients who chose to stop eating and drinking because they were ready to die, saw continued existence as pointless, and considered their quality of life poor." The survey showed that 85 percent of patients died within 15 days of stopping food and fluids. On a scale of 0 (a very bad death) to 9 (a very good death), the median score for the quality of these deaths, as rated by the nurses, was 8.

(https://www.ncbi.nlm.nih.gov/pubmed/12878744)[8]

Allen and Beverly had warning signs, but the Accidental Safari had begun suddenly during the ordinary task of unloading groceries. It had taken them through the emergency room, to a hospital room, a rehabilitation facility, a nursing home, back home and, ultimately, to heaven! The entire journey had taken many long hours, but just nine short weeks.

In spite of the warning signs, Allen and Beverly were unprepared for the Accidental Safari that swept them away. Allen had experienced nagging, undiagnosed medical issues for two years. Sadly, the medical issue that eluded diagnosis and the natural human tendency to deny the situation caught up with them.

This may be a good time for a reality check. Ask yourself. "Have I taken steps to prepare for an active and healthy retirement? What steps can I take to prepare for an Accidental Safari?" Many of us will avoid asking these questions until it is too late. The circle of life never stops turning, so the best time to prepare for the journey is now.

4

PREPARING FOR THE SAFARI

A Safari company in Tanzania offers eight different Safari experiences. With a little advance planning, you can even choose to Safari in a hot air balloon! But, if you wait until you arrive at the airport in Dar es Salaam to contact the tour company, the chances are you will not get your first choice of tour packages. The balloon ride will be sold out, the pilot will be on vacation, or the river will have washed out. Time and circumstances will have limited your options. Similarly, failure to plan ahead for the Accidental Safari may limit your options and impact your ability to navigate successfully.

Before you find yourself in uncharted territory, it is wise to consider the big picture and begin to prepare a plan for the Safari.

THE CRITICAL STEPS OF PREPARATION

Whether this is your journey or you are along for the ride with someone you love, the shock and the fear of traveling an unfamiliar path can be crippling. But the good news is that the paths through the jungle are predictable and, because they are predictable, they can be anticipated. And, if they can be anticipated, you can be prepared. Being informed, organized, and equipped for the journey will not only give you peace of mind but may also give you hope and a healthy perspective of the trails and the trials ahead.

If you are entering into an Accidental Safari, follow these critical preparation steps:

Find an Experienced Guide . If you were going to take an actual Safari, you would probably do extensive research to find an experienced Safari guide. A guide to the Accidental Safari is just as important. Whether you have prepared for an inevitable Safari or have been thrust into one unexpectedly, your first step is to find an experienced guide you can trust. The advice of an expert can help you make the best of the current situation and explain the options that are open to you. You will want to pay close attention to the guide's instructions. He/she should explain all of the options available to you, so you can begin to weigh both the risks and opportunities when deciding which path to take.

Gather relevant information in an organized manner. As you research, collect information in a three-ring binder or file folders (even on your smartphone) and categorize the material as you gather it. As you gain familiarity with the information, you can identify the specific issues that are pertinent. Once the needs have been identified, you can begin to equip yourself.

Equip yourself. Look to your guide to provide an accurate map of the highlights and dangers on the road ahead. As you prepare for your own inevitable Safari, or that of a loved one, confirm your assessment of the care issues and expected problems, and begin to implement the proposed solutions with your guide. Get equipped for the journey by preparing the necessary legal documents to protect yourself and ensure that your needs and wishes are satisfied. This legal documentation is presented in detail in **Chapter 5: May I See Your Papers?**

Choose your care team. When planning a vacation, a preliminary consideration is usually who you want to travel with you. In preparing for an Accidental Safari, you will need to ask yourself the same questions: "Who is dependable and has all the qualities important in a traveling companion? Who would make a good partner? Who would I turn to if I found myself in unfamiliar territory? Who could I depend on if I had to? Who would I trust with my money and my life?"

You will need to carefully consider who you would want on your team if the journey involved fighting for life in an emergency room, a hospital room, a rehabilitation facility, or your own bed. Write down all of the names that come to mind. If the number one person is unavailable, ask yourself who would be your second choice, or your third choice. If these individuals are older than you are, it would be wise to identify one or two people who are younger.

Most people choose their spouse first. But if you are selecting a person who will be an active advocate in seeing that your care needs are met, rather than as a life partner, would your choice be different? The person you married may not be gifted in the areas that will be important when you most need an advocate. This situation is a delicate one, which is why I encourage clients to consider naming multiple co-advocates when they are choosing team members for the Life Care Plan.

If you are running through a preliminary list of names at this moment and are trying to narrow the list, you are a blessed individual. If you have several trustworthy people in mind, you are well on your way to a Life Care Plan.

If you are struggling to think of anyone who would stand by you when an Accidental Safari comes, or if there is no one you would trust with that authority, you are not alone. I discuss this in **Chapter 11: Lions and Tigers, Oh My**.

WHO ME?

If you have been chosen to join the care team of a loved one, or if you are already providing care, you may feel overwhelmed. You may not feel that you have the "gift" of care and fear such a large responsibility. You may have the desire to help, but the patient may live many miles, states, or even countries away.

Remember that not everyone is cut out to be, or able to be, a physical caregiver. Some individuals may serve best as a care manager, as the person who handles the elder's finances, or as the person who takes the senior shopping or brings the groceries. All of these roles have value. If many hands make light work, then we share in the blessings as we share the work.

Think about what is most important in the relationship you have or have had with the person needing care: your shared history, lasting memories, and genuine love for him/ her. It is wonderful if you can provide some of the services that are needed, but the truth is your primary contribution may be in just being there, loving, and respecting him/her.

If you feel overwhelmed today with the physical tasks of care giving, seek help. If you are in a relationship with someone who is overwhelmed by the tasks and needs help but refuses to accept it, step in as best you can, despite their stubborn refusals. I want to encourage you to "keep on keeping on." Your labor will inspire others to do likewise if you tell them what you are doing and invite them to help you. By doing so, you will be helping to increase awareness of the needs of the elderly, and it may gain you some welcome assistance. Caring for someone is labor, but it brings a blessing in the satisfaction and joy that comes from giving.

BE TRUE TO YOURSELF

Finally, if you believe that there is a certain therapy, treatment, or drug that may provide an answer to your situation, you may feel compelled to follow a particular treatment against the advice of your doctor. Similarly, if a loved one you are caring for wants to veer from the recommended path, you may need to support the decision, even if you don't agree with it. It is important to acknowledge the inherent risk of any treatment, whether conventional or unconventional. Keep an open dialogue about the possible motivations and expectations.

CREATING A LIFE CARE PLAN

Sadly, many of the people destined for an Accidental Safari will be traveling alone. The Baby Boomers, born between 1946 and 1964, had smaller families than their parents had. Some of them have no families at all; they may be divorced, widowed, or never married. These factors have created a large population of "elder orphans": seniors without family connections, few close friends, and no one to advocate for, or support, them.

The Baby Boomer generation was born at the end of World War II, when a generation of young men and women returned from war to start families. (Learn more about this generation by watching the online video at http://www.history.com/topics/baby-boomers). When the babies began to arrive, it triggered a rippling wave of unmet needs. The wave that began in 1946 resulted in the need to increase the number of hospital delivery rooms. It was followed by an increased need for homes, kindergarten classrooms, high schools, and colleges. Today, the Boomers' needs are for in-home care services, assisted living facilities, and nursing homes. These expanded needs have led to an explosion in the industries that serve seniors. These industries are working overtime to meet the demands, not only for new buildings, but for the personnel to staff them.

Boomers are advised to be as prepared as possible for an inevitable Safari. Unfortunately, the statistics show that most of them are not prepared. They have spent more time and money planning for kitchen remodels than planning for the long-term care, legal, and financial issues that come with aging.

So how do we begin to prepare? Some people are natural planners, and others are not. If you have an earthquake emergency kit under your bed; a roadside emergency kit in the trunk of your car; and water, dried food, a first aid kit, and a battery-operated radio in the basement, you are a planner.

When you were expecting your first child, did you pack a suitcase for the inevitable "run to the hospital"? Since aging is also inevitable, we will be wise to prepare for it by developing a plan.

Statistics show that all of us will need care at some time in our lives. "Seventy percent of people turning age 65 can expect to use some form of long-term care during their lives." (http://longtermcare.gov/the-basics/who-needs-care.html)[9]

This doesn't mean that you should wait until you are 65 to begin building the emergency kit. I recommend that you start with the two parts of the plan that should be addressed as early as possible: the care in the plan and the cost of the plan. We will deal with the "care in the plan" first. The "cost of the plan" is discussed in **Chapter 6: Financing the Journey**.

THE CARE IN THE PLAN

The Accidental Safari is not a short-term adventure. It requires "care-ful" planning, beginning with an assessment of the personal resources that will be needed and available to you. This issue is one I addressed recently with one of my clients:

AN ELDER ORPHAN

Alice was 79 years old and had been a widow for many years. She lived in the Clearview Apartments, a development of about 50 small duplexes built with Housing and Urban Development (HUD) funds. It was rent subsidized and exclusively for folks over the age of 55. The community was within walking distance of a shopping mall. It was an ideal senior community, with a manager and people who intentionally looked out for one another.

When I explained to Alice that a Power of Attorney document would allow her to appoint someone who would have the legal authority to assist her with finances and medical issues, she just looked at me with a blank expression. She finally said, "I can't think of anyone to name." She and her husband, Peter, had moved to the area after Peter retired. When Peter died unexpectedly, she didn't really have a support network in place. She said, "After Peter passed away, I tried to stay in the house, but it was too much for me. I can't think of anyone to name. What do people like me do?"

I asked her the obvious questions.

"Do you have any children?"

"No."

"Nieces or nephews?"

"No."

I continued asking questions: Friends? Neighbors? Groups you belong to? A church? Other interests?

"None close to me. None that I would want to know my business. No. No. Not really," she answered.

I approached from a different angle. "Who would be the beneficiary of your estate when you die?"

"I'm not sure; maybe the humane society."

"If the majority of your estate is going to a charity, you could name a representative of the charity to be the executor of your estate, but that still doesn't answer the immediate questions: Who can step in while you are alive to be your advocate? Who's got your back and can make sure your plans are carried out? Who could you name in your Powers of Attorney for asset management and health care?"

Alice had no immediate answer. She could not identify one person in her life that she felt close enough to call upon. We had to dig deeper into the options available to elder orphans to find a choice that would be acceptable to her.

So what can people like Alice do to build a care team? First, know that you are not alone. God loves and cares about you. Second, there are many reasons why you may be unable to choose a care partner. You may have elected to be alone in life. You may feel that you have no one you can turn to because you have made some poor life choices. Perhaps life has dealt you a bad hand, or you have been hurt by someone you trusted. Know that there is healing for past hurts as you reach out to touch others. You may fear reaching out, but it is important that you begin to look around for others in a similar situation who may also need a care partner.

Take the opportunity to reach out. Many organizations in your community would welcome your involvement and help. You can also begin to look for a situation that would allow you to act in the position of helper for someone else. The helper has more control and is not as vulnerable or exposed as the person receiving the help. Reaching out could be as easy as offering to care for a neighbor's pet or sitting with someone who is shut in and needs companionship. Grace is an example of an elder-orphan who has built a community by reaching out.

ALONE YET NOT ALONE

Grace loved to sing and could do so very well. She was a "shut in" because her physical condition made it very difficult for her to get out of the house. Determined not to be lonely, Grace called a friend, Katie, and asked if she could sing Katie a song. Katie was delighted! Katie asked Grace to call again at any time to sing another song. The calls and songs became a regular routine for Grace and Katie. One day, Katie mentioned to a friend that she looked forward to the calls/songs from Grace. Katie's friend asked her if she thought she could also receive calls/songs from Grace. Before long, Grace had a list of people whose days were brightened by her regular singing phone calls.

Early selection of a care team is important because your advocates must be legally authorized to step in and act on your behalf at the onset of an Accidental Safari. This type of Safari does not require an advance reservation. It can begin at any time. Therefore, your traveling companions need to be selected and authorized before the emergency hits.

After identifying a list of possible care partners, contact each of them and ask if they would consider joining your care team. It is best if they have agreed to serve, and are prepared to serve, before the first call for help. Tell them why you have chosen them. Tell them that you appreciate them and that you trust them. Tell them what your expectations are and ask if they have any questions or concerns. Ask them if they have any suggestions as to how things could work and if they know of anyone else who might be of assistance.

Initiating a conversation with your advocates opens the door for future conversations about your needs and expectations. Suddenly there is permission to talk about delicate issues that were formerly off-limits.

Prepare a three-ring binder that will become your Life Care Book. The Life Care Book will contain information on everything related to your care needs, such as the list of medications you take, your financial and healthcare Powers of Attorney, Advance Health Directives, and prepaid funeral arrangements.

Powers of Attorney, Advance Health Directives to Physicians (also called Living Wills), and Physician Orders for Life-Sustaining Treatment (POLST), are documents that can be used to legally authorize trusted individuals to act on your behalf when help is needed. Under the current Health Privacy

Act, even a spouse must be authorized, in writing, to discuss your case with a medical professional, have your records transferred to an alternate physician for a second opinion, or make an appointment for you with your doctor.

Once you have identified your care team and have the legal documents in place that authorize them to act on your behalf, you should create a Life Care Plan that reflects what you have determined to be the essential, important, and preferred action steps to be taken should you find yourself on an Accidental Safari.

A Life Care Plan should anticipate and address each of the stages of the journey. The itinerary for an Accidental Safari typically begins with an unplanned and unexpected departure from the common activities of life, prompted by out-of-control medical issues and care needs. The increasing need for care leads to a housing crisis. The care and housing issues generally lead to significant financial challenges, and the options available at that point will be entirely dependent on the ability to financially meet these costs of care and housing.

All the moving parts of the Life Care Plan should be addressed in detail. The key is to be aware of the issues and the consequences, to determine the level of detail your plan should include. How far you go down the trail to plan and prepare will depend on what it takes to give you peace of mind that these issues have been taken care of adequately. The amount of resources, time, money, and emotional effort you want to spend is up to you.

> Develop a Life Care Book, a place to gather all the bits of information that will eventually come together to form your Individual Life Care Plan!

A FAILURE TO PLAN

People generally fail to plan for one of three reasons: denial, procrastination, or apathy.

Denial. I occasionally get a phone call from someone who is close to death. They are calling because, in the eleventh hour, they want to create a plan. Unfortunately, when death is imminent, you no longer need a Life Care Plan. You need a plan for death.

Procrastination. Sometimes I get a phone call from a person who wants an emergency Last Will and Testament written because they are taking an overseas trip. The trip, which they have been planning for many months, is just a little outside their comfort zone, and, just days before they leave, they are hoping to get the peace of mind that comes from having their legal affairs in order. Having a plan in place before traveling is always a good idea, but it won't happen if the plane leaves early Saturday morning and they wait until Thursday afternoon to call me. Procrastination is a failure to plan.

Apathy. Apathy is the primary reason why fewer than fifty percent of the populace have executed a Last Will and Testament. It is also the reason that Life Care Planning has a low priority. But, sadly, the reality is that most of us will find ourselves on an Accidental Safari at some time in our lives, and most will be unprepared for it.

If you are approaching retirement, someone close to you is sick or has died, you are taking a trip, or you are just getting a little older, I encourage you to start gathering information and take action to develop a Life Care Plan.

SUSTAINABILITY

Two key questions to ask when preparing your Life Care Plan are: "Will the plan meet its defined purpose over the long term?" and "Can the plan be sustained?"

Sustainability is especially important. Merriam-Webster defines the word "sustainable" as "able to be used without being completely used up or destroyed; able to last or continue for a long time."

Two elements that will affect the sustainability of the plan are cost and commitment. The plan *can't* be pursued if there is no way to pay for it. The plan *won't* be pursued if there is a lack of commitment to it. Whatever path you choose to take, you will want to choose one that you can and will follow to the finish line. Ensuring that your plan is sustainable will require you to carefully consider the potential impact on your finances, housing, and desire for independence. These issues will be discussed in detail in the chapters that follow.

5

MAY I SEE YOUR PAPERS?

We have all seen movies where the hero is seen approaching an enemy border checkpoint, or his train is stopped and heavily armed guards are moving down the center aisle checking passengers' papers. We get the unspoken message that if you don't have your papers in order, bad things are going to happen.

In America, the closest we get to this is when we are pulled over for a traffic infraction. We reach for our driver's license, registration, and insurance cards, which must be at hand and in order. Without them, we are certain to get a citation.

On the Accidental Safari, if you don't have the right papers, at hand and in order, bad things can and will happen.

WHILE YOU LIVE

The right papers at the right time are important, even critical. The legal documents necessary to pass through the Life Care checkpoints are:

- Powers of Attorney

- Advance Health Directive to Physicians (Living Will)
- Last Will and Testament

A Power of Attorney (POA) is a document that authorizes someone to act for you, to figuratively 'stand in your shoes,' when you need something done but are unable to do it for yourself for any reason. This person will be your named agent, also called an "attorney-in-fact" (not a licensed attorney). The POA will also enumerate the specific powers or authority granted to your agent on your behalf.

A Power of Attorney is typically titled as a "General Durable Power of Attorney." Let's consider each of these terms specifically. The term "general" means that the document conveys broad powers covering nearly every possible circumstance or condition. An alternate form of power of attorney, called a "Limited Power of Attorney," gives the named agent limited authority to accomplish only a specific task or tasks outlined in the document, or within a limited period of time.

For example, if I was going to take a short trip, I could give you a Limited Power of Attorney that authorizes you to sign (for me) closing documents on the purchase of a piece of property on a particular date. You could not use that document to conduct any other business for me, and your authority to act on my behalf is limited by the terms of the document. If I was going to be out of the country for six months, I could name you as my agen, in a Limited Power of Attorney that authorizes you to act for me in any financial capacity necessary but only for the period of time specified. Therefore, the Limited Power of Attorney can limit the scope or the time of the powers.

The term "durable" means that the authority being conveyed will continue to be in effect even if the principal (the person who executed the document) becomes incapacitated or incompetent. Historically, Powers of Attorney would remain in effect only so long as the principal was competent. So, in years past, if I left town, my named agent could act for me as directed in the POA until I returned and could once again act for myself. But, if I fell off my horse on the way home and was injured and unable to act, the agent named in the Power of Attorney would also not be able to act, because I was not able to act for myself. Given the speed of travel and communication today, the original intent no longer makes sense. So, Powers of Attorney were given a durability clause which authorizes the agent to act for the principal even when the principal becomes incapacitated or incompetent.

If you become incapacitated and need help to carry out routine personal, medical, or financial tasks, someone must be appointed and authorized to step in and act with you or for you. Who gets to decide who that individual will be? If you have executed a Power of Attorney before an injury or disease renders you incapable, you have decided. But without a properly executed (signed and notarized) legal Power of Attorney, a court (through the process of guardianship or conservatorship) will choose the best person to manage your physical and financial affairs.

Guardianships and conservatorships are time consuming and costly court procedures that can be entirely avoided if you have simply executed a Power of Attorney naming an individual to act for you in the event of an emergency. Let's imagine that you have suffered a head injury and are incapacitated and unable to act temporarily. You cannot write checks or conduct business and cannot make emergency medical decisions for yourself. If you have a Power of Attorney in place, your named agent would be authorized to take such actions on your behalf.

If you have not executed a Power of Attorney, no one would be empowered to act on your behalf, and a court would need to appoint a temporary guardian who could act for you. In a Guardianship Action, the court will decide who can make decisions regarding an incapacitated person's physical and/or financial affairs. A guardian may be authorized by the court to take control of an incapacitated person's medical and personal needs. That individual (or agency) is called the guardian or conservator of the person. If the court appoints a guardian of the incapacitated person's finances, that individual is called the guardian of the estate. The guardian of the person and the guardian of the estate are usually the same person (or agency), called the guardian of the person and the estate.

The court will decide if the alleged incapacitated person needs limited help in the area of finances and/or personal and medical needs and may grant a limited guardianship. In the case of a limited guardianship, the court will be very specific as to the powers of the guardian as well as the limitations on the powers of the guardian and/or the incapacitated person.

In the past, Powers of Attorney used to deal with both financial and medical issues in a single document, for convenience sake. Today, it is common to have two individual documents: a Power of Attorney for Asset Management (POA-AM) for financial matters and a Power of Attorney for Healthcare (POA-

HC). The passing of the Health Insurance Portability and Accountability Act of 1996 (HIPAA) required specific language to be added to the POA-HC that grants access by the named agent to the principal's medical information that, because of HIPAA, became privacy protected, even between spouses.

In discussing Powers of Attorney for Healthcare with clients, I occasionally have someone say, "I have a Healthcare Power of Attorney from the (local) clinic. You won't need to prepare one of those." I will then ask him/her if that Power of Attorney contains a paragraph that allows the agent to fire the doctor at will or to check the patient out of the hospital against medical advice, or if it requires the health agency to provide copies of all of the patients' medical records to the agent?

In my experience, the forms offered by a health service provider at no cost, such as a clinic connected to your health insurance provider, have been carefully written to make it easy for you to cooperate with the organization and comply with their policies. As the Safari guide, it is my job to tell you what you need to know and give you the tools you'll need to get things done the way you want them to be done.

When it's "crunch time," you don't want to be blindsided by the fine print, or the lack of it, in a document that favors the institution over the patient. These "fill in the blank" forms may be better than nothing, but they can come back and bite you at the wrong time in a big way. It's a jungle out there and, depending on the circumstances, it may be as important to be armed with mosquito repellant as with a high-powered rifle.

On the other hand, it is not uncommon for clients to tell me that they want a "simple" Power of Attorney. They'll point out a particular paragraph in the document and ask, "Why does this have to be in there?" My typical response is "It may not need to be in there, unless at some time in the future you need it to be in there, and then it needs to be in there." No one can predict the future with certainty, so you will need a document broad enough to cover most situations.

A Power of Attorney is a critical document to have during your lifetime because it is only effective (valid) while you are alive. At your death, the POA becomes null and void. Upon death, your Last Will and Testament will assert control; directing how things are to be done and who has the authority to do them.

Two primary questions to answer when executing a POA are: "Who?" and "When?" If you already have a POA in place, I suggest that you find it and carefully review it to answer the following questions:

Who is named as the agent/attorney-in-fact? Is the agent still the one you would want to have power to act for you? Do you have an alternate agent named if your first choice is unable to serve?

When is the POA effective? Is the document effective (valid) now? Does something need to happen before the document becomes effective and the agent empowered to act? When can it be used by the agent? There should be a paragraph that states when the document is valid to use, whether it is effective at the time it was signed or at some time in the future. It may state that it is effective only upon your incapacity or incompetence and that a state of incompetence must be evidenced by a certified letter from your treating physician or possibly two concurring physicians. Securing a written determination letter from a doctor that you are incompetent to act on your own behalf can be very inconvenient, even difficult. Securing one from two doctors can be nearly impossible. In my opinion, most Powers of Attorney for elderly persons should become effective immediately at the time the POA is executed (signed), so that a doctor visit, a diagnosis, and a determination letter (of incapacity or incompetency) is not necessary. In fact, an elderly person may not be incompetent at all, but it may be more convenient for the agent to act in his or her stead. Carol, encountered some of these issues with the Powers of Attorney for her husband, Jack.

COMMON SENSE

Carol came to see me carrying a large binder over-flowing with estate planning documents executed just four months earlier. She had been busy contact-ing memory care facilities to locate a bed for her hus-band, Jack, who was suffering from dementia. Caring for Jack at home had become too much for Carol. A friend suggested that she bring the documents to me, for review.

Jack had signed all of the documents. His signature was rough, but legal. The problem was that the Power of Attorney Jack had executed stated that before Carol could act as his attorney-in-fact under the Power of Attorney for Asset Management (POA-AM) for financial matters, Carol needed letters from two physicians stating that Jack was incompetent and unable to manage his own affairs.

From an elder law perspective, some issues require just a little basic common sense. I cannot imagine drafting a Power of Attorney that would require a determination letter of incompetency from two physicians for a client who needed an agent who could use the POA immediately! Carol's husband clearly needed immediate help, and the POA he signed just four short months ago should have accounted for that.

I gave Carol a list of the changes I recommended be made to her estate planning documents that would offer significant and immediate help to both of them. I sent her back to the original attorney with the advice that she should expect the corrections to be made at no charge.

Before she left my office, Carol admitted to me that prior to coming to the appointment, out of curiosity, she had contacted the original law firm anonymously and asked if they practiced elder law. The person on the other end of the phone told her that the firm did not practice elder law and recommended that she call me.

It is very important to choose an attorney who is experienced in the areas in which you need help. You wouldn't go to a general practitioner for heart surgery or to a podiatrist for skin cancer. If you have problems related to aging or incapacity, find an elder law attorney who handles Powers of Attorney and Special Needs Trusts. Interview more than one, if necessary, to find someone you have confidence in.

Mental incompetency is generally not a sudden occurrence. Symptoms may appear as the result of a bad day, a bad week, or even a bad month. They might be brought on by a change in medication or a urinary tract infection. Any one of these issues can be the reason for the appearance of diminished mental capacity. Some of these issues can mean a permanent disability, while others create a temporary disability. But it will always be time consuming, inconvenient, and expensive to get a doctor's letter of incompetency in order to authorize the use of a Power of Attorney. And the entire process would be unnecessary if the Power of Attorney is written to be effective immediately!

Is there a downside? Perhaps. If the POA becomes effective immediately upon execution, the named agent could use it at any time, and there is always the possibility that he/she might use it improperly. A few practical steps can be taken to reduce the fear and bring peace of mind in this situation:

Choose someone you trust. You should only choose an agent or agents that you know to be honest and responsible. Someone who keeps his/her own finances in order and balances his/her own checkbook would be preferable.

Equip the agent(s). Inform the agent(s) of your expectations as to his/her duties. Remind them that an agent has a legal and fiduciary responsibility which holds them personally responsible for any intentional misconduct or self-serving actions. I suggest that you do not give the agent a copy of the POA until you actually need his/her assistance.

Name co-agents. Co-agents become more important the older you get. Most couples will choose each other to act as the agent/attorney-in-fact. It's important to remember, however, that your spouse is aging at the same rate that you are. So, it is entirely possible that around the time your aches and pains are catching up with you, or dementia is creeping in, your spouse may be suffering from similar issues. Each of you may be hoping that the other one of you will take care of some pressing matter. If your POA is effective only upon your incapacity, you will have to go to the doctor's office to get the letter that says you are not competent to manage your affairs. If the POA is effective immediately, but names only your spouse as agent, and your spouse is unable to rise to the occasion, your spouse will have to resign as your agent. Alternatively, you could get a letter from the doctor stating that your spouse is incompetent, so the successor agent can step up to replace him/her.

It is always a good idea to widen your circle of wise counsel. I am personally in favor of naming co-agents (who can act separately) on Powers of Attorney. Co-agents are accountable to each other. In the situation above, if you had named an individual to act as a co-agent (meaning "with equal power") with your spouse, that person could have stepped in to act for you immediately. No one would have had to go to the doctor's office. Letters declaring incompetence would not be required. Some attorneys advise against naming co-agents because they fear it will sow seeds of revolution. I concede that if you ask two of your children, who have hated each other from birth, to share this power and responsibility as co-agents, things will probably not go well. I also don't recommend naming the "black sheep" of the family, who has just left a drug rehab center to move home and help take care of mom and dad, as a co-agent with your spouse. That scenario is not likely to end well, either.

On the other hand, two people who will accept the fiduciary responsibility, and who get along with each other and genuinely care for you, can make a wonderful team. As co-agents, they can help each other. They can work out an arrangement that maximizes their individual strengths. There is an increased, and very real, sense of accountability when two people work together that is absent when a single individual is given all of the authority of an attorney-in-fact.

Accountability is extremely important, not just in financial matters but in the everyday issues and decisions of life. If an elderly couple act as sole agents for each other, and they are both experiencing a decline in mental acuity, they are vulnerable to the potential scams and abuse discussed in **Chapter 11: Lions and Tigers, Oh My**.

Name a successor agent. If you have named a sole agent (or co-agents), your POA should also name an alternate (or successor) agent, if the current agent or one of the co-agents is unable to serve. The attorney-in-fact does not have the authority to name his/her successor; therefore, you must appoint an alternate in the POA. If you are appointing co-agents, you should name one or more alternate agents to replace the initial agents if one or both become unable to serve.

Before a successor agent can act, he or she will need to show proof that the initial (or prior acting) agent cannot or will not continue to serve. This evidence must be provided to the bank, business, physician, or hospital, etc. to show that the transfer of authority as attorney-in-fact has occurred following the terms of the POA. This proof can be in the form of a death certificate (if the prior attorney-in-fact is deceased), a notarized letter of resignation from the acting attorney-in-fact, or a letter from a physician indicating that the named agent is no longer competent to serve. This written confirmation, which states the reason the current agent is unable to continue serving, authorizes the successor agent to assume the power to act.

If you have named co-agents, you have several options for filling a vacancy if one of the initial co-agents ceases to serve. First, the surviving initial co-agent could continue to serve alone as sole agent. You could also have the alternate agent step in as a successor co-agent with the surviving initial co-agent. The alternate agent might also step in as successor sole agent only at such time as both of the original co-agents can no longer serve. These are important decisions that need to be made when the POA is being drafted.

Your Powers of Attorney for Healthcare and Asset Management are a vital part of your "papers." They are as essential to the Accidental Safari as a passport, visa, driver's license, and shot record are to an African Safari. The POA allows your advocate to step in to help you when you need help and will continue to be in effect until it is revoked or you die. By law, a POA automatically becomes void at your death.

APPROACHING DEATH

As you near the end of life, you will need to have three additional documents in place:

- Physicians Orders for Life Sustaining Treatment (POLST)

- Advance Health Directive to Physicians/Living Will (AHD)

- Instructions for Palliative Care (PC)

Physician Orders for Life-Sustaining Treatment (POLST). A POLST is easily-recognized. It is a standardized, portable, brightly colored single sheet that documents a conversation between a medical provider and a patient who is nearing the end of life. The pragmatic rule for medical clinicians is to initiate a conversation about POLST when a patient is expected to die within one year.

"POLST" stands for Physician Orders for Life-Sustaining Treatment. It addresses those situations where emergency medical intervention is being considered. The form directs how the emergency medical personnel should respond if there are no signs of life (neither pulse nor breathing). It states a patient's specific wishes regarding attempted resuscitation. For example, the form allows the patient to stipulate that in specific circumstances (such as where there is a pulse and/or breathing), the patient would want comfort measures only to be given, some limited additional interventions, or full restorative treatment. The form also directs, in non-emergency situations, whether the patient would want antibiotics or a feeding tube to be administered.

TO POLST OR NOT TO POLST?

In a recent consultation, a client explained to me that she did not need an Advance Health Directive to Physicians because she already had a POLST.

"Why do you have a POLST?" I asked.

"Because my doctor said that I should have one."

"Well, you look healthy to me, is there something going on that you would need a POLST?"

"Well, I'm 86 years old," she said with a twinkle in her eye.

I smiled and said, "The years have been good to you. If you keeled over this afternoon I would call 9-1-1 and you would probably want me to."

She nodded.

We went on the have a discussion about the difference between a POLST and the Advance Health Directive to Physicians.

Advance Health Directive to Physicians (AHD). In an AHD, the client has described the circumstances under which specific actions should be carried out. The attorney-in-fact named in the client's Power of Attorney for Healthcare (POA-HC) is authorized to make these decisions. The directive requires a medical evaluation of the client's condition and a consultation between the attorney-in-fact and the doctor before the directives can be followed. This means that everything will be done to save you, stabilize you, and transport you to the hospital for a diagnosis and consultation before the decisions regarding such things as continuing or ending life support procedures will be made. The situation Ralph and Mary faced illustrates how the AHD works:

DIFFICULT DECISIONS

Ralph and Mary came to me for a basic estate plan when they were in their middle years. They each signed an Advance Health Directive to Physicians. The directive outlined this scenario: If the client is unable to communicate, and the attorney-in-fact and physician agree that death is imminent with no hope of recovery, the directive's instructions are to be followed.

Both Ralph and Mary indicated that, under these circumstances, where death was imminent, they would not want a feeding tube to provide artificial nutrition, would not want an IV to provide artificial hydration, would not want attempted resuscitation if their heart had stopped, and would not want to be placed on life support through a ventilator. However, they would want pain medication to prevent suffering.

A few years after Ralph and Mary executed their estate plan, Mary was diagnosed with cancer. She was failing quickly, and her doctor requested a meeting with Ralph.

Ralph told me later that he was terrified to meet with the doctor. "I was so afraid he was going to ask me what I wanted to do. I knew what I wanted. God, did I know what I wanted. But the doctor looked at me and asked a different question. He asked, "What would Mary want us to do?" That was a very different question, because I knew what she would want. We had spoken about it, and I had a directive that she signed that said what she wanted if death was imminent. It was not at all what I wanted, but I could do what she wanted me to do." He presented the doctor with the directive, and her wishes regarding end-of-life treatment were followed.

Both the POLST and the Advance Health Directive to Physicians (AHD) address end-of-life issues. However, while the POLST gives direction to emergency medical personnel, the AHD provides information about the client's wishes and identifies who has the authority to decide what medical actions, emergency or otherwise, should be applied in a given situation. The attorney-in-fact named in a Power of Attorney for Healthcare should be the decision maker.

The POLST is important if you have a progressive, debilitating disease or a terminal diagnosis and your prayer is that if God doesn't heal you that He will take you quickly. If one of your prayers is answered and you get to die quickly, you do not want a first responder to do their job and try to bring you back. The POLST is your physician speaking, under your authority, to instruct the EMT to treat you according to the wishes dictated by the form.

The major difference between the POLST and the Directive to Physicians is that the POLST spells out the patient's pre-determined course of action (moving to allow death if certain conditions exist) and a physician has confirmed that choice in advance of a major medical event. If the patient's plan is toward life, a POLST is not necessary, because emergency medical personnel will always act to save life, stabilize the patient, and transport him/her to the hospital. Clients sometimes ask me where they should keep the POLST. I suggest that they staple the POLST to the chest, so when Emergency Medical Technicians rip open the shirt, they'll see that brightly colored form and stop dead in their tracks.

By making the difficult end-of-life decisions early, you have empowered the attorney-in-fact to act with confidence when the time comes, in a manner that reflects your own expressed wishes. To be effective, the Advance Health Directive to Physicians may require an agreement between the attorney-in-fact and the doctor that there is no hope of recovery. My clients typically express a desire that the final authority to make these decisions rest in the hands of a particular family member or friend named as their agent in the POA-HC with whom they have discussed these matters. If the family continues to hope for a miracle, the AHD is not ready to be asserted.

If you are admitted to the hospital for a procedure of any kind, you will be asked to provide a copy of your Power of Attorney for Healthcare and a copy of your Advance Health

Directive to Physicians. I encourage all my clients to provide a copy of the Power of Attorney for Healthcare to both the doctor and the hospital, but not the AHD. The client should alert the doctor and the hospital to the fact that they have an AHD and give instructions on how the attorney-in-fact can be reached if life-and-death decisions must be made. The AHD should remain in the hands of the agent only, because he/she will be the only one with the authority to assert the directives when the time comes. Neither the hospital nor the doctor will be tasked with the job of making the end-of-life decisions. They just need to know who to call. If a client's heart stopped beating on the operating table, I would not want someone in the operating room to see the checked box on the AHD that called for "no resuscitation" and announce "Let's go to lunch." I want the medical team to do everything in their collective power to save my client until such time as my client or his/her agent can direct otherwise!

The AHD addresses certain specific end-of-life circumstances that are required by state statute. It can also include scenarios that the client and the attorney may feel are relevant and helpful. The client can also tailor the AHD to address specific areas of fear or concern that the client may have. As the following examples illustrate, a tailored AHD can be very specific.

A CANDY BAR, A FLASHLIGHT, AND A CELL PHONE

Once while I was discussing the Advance Health Directive to Physicians (AHD), a client told me that she wanted me to put into her AHD that she wanted to be buried with a cell phone, a candy bar, and a flashlight. There was a long pause. Then she smiled at me and said, "I'm kidding . . . sort of."

Another client asked that her AHD include the "Hawaiian pizza test." She said, "If I have been lying in bed and I am unresponsive, take a warm slice of Hawaiian pizza and wave it slowly under my nose. If there is still no response, pull the plug. Life is not worth living!"

The POA-HC identifies the person or persons (agent/co-agents) who has the final authority to assert the AHD. The AHD stipulates the conditions under which the Directive is asserted. For example, these conditions could include a number of convergent issues:

- When death is imminent

- When the injury, disease, or illness is terminal

- When the client is unable to communicate his/her wishes

- When the application of life support would not save the patient's life but serve only to prolong death

The AHD may stipulate that the agent act in consultation with the physician on certain matters. Be warned, however, that requiring a joint decision will force the parties to reach agreement or do nothing. In a sense, both parties can hold the other hostage. The attorney-in-fact might be ready to follow the AHD, but the doctor may prefer to wait a little longer. Or perhaps the family is holding out for a miracle, but the doctor is pushing for end-of-life measures. What happens?

In my opinion, there is wise counsel with many advisors, so I can see the logic in naming more than one individual to make these important, but difficult decisions. Realistically, however, there must be a final decision maker, or a process that allows for a final decision to be made if the situation reaches a stalemate. In that situation, it will come down to the person the client chose to hold the power and have the final word. These are important factors to discuss when the AHD is drafted.

If a client wants the attorney-in-fact to have the final decision-making power, but also wants the doctor to participate in the decision, the AHD could state that it is the client's wish that decisions be made jointly by both the attorney-in-fact and the doctor, but in the absence of an agreement between the parties, name one or the other as the final decision maker. The client may stipulate that the attorney-in-fact would have the authority to remove the doctor if, in the opinion of the attorney-in-fact, it becomes necessary to find a new doctor to move forward. Similarly, the Power of Attorney could specifically bar the attorney-in-fact from removing the doctor if the client wants to ensure that the doctor will continue to participate in the process.

The AHD may require that the patient be unable to communicate before it can be implemented. A terminal patient, who is still able to communicate, can still direct his or her own care. However, when a terminal patient is unable to communicate, that is when the AHD must do the talking.

In 1990, Terri Schiavo suffered a cardiac arrest which left her in a vegetative state. In 1998, her husband filed a petition in Florida District Court to have her feeding tube removed, which would result in her death. The case went through the court system for seven additional years, with many appeals. Ultimately, Terri's feeding tube was ordered removed by the court, and she died in 2005. Issues in this case included whether or not Terri had any brain activity and to what extent she may have expressed her wishes should she ever be in such a condition. Terri had left no written AHD, so the court made the end-of-life decision for her.

If Terri Schiavo had executed an Advance Health Directive to Physicians containing instructions about what she would have wanted if she was ever "in a permanent unconscious condition," it would have been much easier for the involved parties to reach agreement on the best course of action. Because she did not have an AHD, Terri Schiavo's death became a national tragedy. The good news is her story drew widespread attention to the benefits of an Advance Health Directive that can speak for us when we cannot.

If you are opposed to the use of medical life-support systems to prolong life, your Advance Health Directive to Physicians should contain the following language set forth by the Revised Code of Washington or other states statutes: "If, at any time, I should be diagnosed in writing to be in a terminal condition by the attending physician or in a permanent unconscious condition by two physicians, and where the application of life-sustaining treatment would serve only to artificially prolong the process of my death, I direct that such treatment be withheld or withdrawn, and that I be permitted to die naturally." *Revised Code of Washington RCW 70.122.030*

This is a delicate issue, and I have seen a wide range of perspectives and emotions when it comes to discussing the end-of-life directive. I have had several clients moved to the point of tears by memories of the death of loved ones. Clients have even become angry when they remembered a time when a loved one's wishes were ignored and life-saving measures were applied, although the loved one had expressed a desire for a natural death. For some clients, the need to make a decision now, for a scenario that likely won't play out for many years to come, is daunting.

Palliative Care. Palliative care (pronounced pal-lee-uh-tiv) is specialized medical care for people with a serious illness. It is focused on providing relief from the symptoms and stress of a serious illness. The goal of palliative care is to improve quality of life for both the patient and the family.

Palliative care is provided by a specially trained team of doctors, nurses, and other specialists who work together with a patient's other doctors to provide an extra layer of support. It is appropriate at any age and at any stage in a serious illness, and it can be provided along with curative treatment.

AFTER DEATH

Disposition of Remains. Another important decision to make in advance of a health crisis is whether you prefer earth burial or cremation. If you aren't sure what you want or haven't communicated your wishes to your spouse or an advocate, how do you expect them to make this important decision with confidence that they are doing exactly what you would want? Decisions concerning the disposition of physical remains can be a big deal and, if they are not addressed in advance, they can become a problem. It is not unusual for a person's remains to be held in cold storage at the funeral home while the adult children of the deceased fight over whether the remains would be cremated or buried.

State law in Washington that addresses the disposition of remains allows you to make your wishes for the handling of your remains known by a directive in writing, signed by you and witnessed. You can find a similar statute on "disposition of remains," in your particular state.

Without a written directive or prepaid arrangements filed with a licensed funeral or cemetery authority, there is a statutory order of priority of who is authorized to make funeral arrangement decisions and pay for them. The following list is the order of priority in the state of Washington for who will decide what happens to your physical remains if you have not left instructions:

Revised Code of Washington, RCW 68.50.160
Right to Disposition of Remains:

1. The person designated by the decedent as authorized to direct disposition as listed on the decedent's United States Department of Defense Record of Emergency Data, DD form 93, or its successor form, if the decedent died while serving in military;

2. The designated agent of the decedent as directed through a written document signed and dated by the decedent in the presence of a witness. The direction of the designated agent is sufficient to direct the type, place, and method of disposition;

3. If there is no written directive, the order is

    a. The surviving spouse;

    b. The majority of the surviving adult children of the decedent;

    c. The surviving parents of the decedent;

    d. The majority of the surviving siblings of the decedent;

    e. A court-appointed guardian for the person at the time of the person's death.

WHO DECIDES?

Who gets to make these important and emotional decisions about health and finance, life and death, and burial or cremation? The answer is "You do." But only if you take action before it's needed. The process is an acknowledgement and contemplation of our mortality, as well as the value and dignity of life. This process takes effort and courage, but it provides a sense of closure and inward satisfaction. Taking care of necessary business always brings peace of mind.

A word to the wise: Get your papers in order before the Accidental Safari begins!

(http://ap.leg/wa.gov/RCW/default.aspx?cite=68.50.160)[10]

6

FINANCING THE JOURNEY

Planning ahead for the Accidental Safari is the best way to ensure that you will have access to all the available options. And nowhere is this more important than when considering the options available for financing the journey.

WHO'S GOING TO PAY FOR ALL THIS?

People typically fall into one of three categories when it comes to paying for the Accidental Safari.

Self-Insured. People who are self-insured intend to pay the costs of long-term care for themselves. They have reached this conclusion either by assessing their financial resources and genetic history and/or deciding that they are financially able to pay their way. They may have decided to roll the dice and risk that the costs will not exceed their resources. Self-insured people also include those who are self-insured by default because they haven't given the matter a thought.

Insured. These people have the financial risk associated with the costs of care covered by Long Term Care (LTC) Insurance. Statistics show that less than 10% of Americans have made this choice.

Uninsured. This category represents the vast majority of Americans who are unaware that Long Term Care Insurance is available, are uninsurable for health reasons, or simply do not have the financial resources to pay for insurance for any part of the Accidental Safari. Both purse and person are fully exposed to the dangers of the journey. An experienced guide can assist you in evaluating the financial impact of an Accidental Safari and the various options available to you for protecting your assets. You may want to ask for a recommendation to an insurance professional who can walk you through the various insurance products available to cover the potential costs of long-term care. An insurance specialist should be well versed in all of the options and be able to make recommendations based on your personal situation and the myriad of other factors that need to be considered.

THE HOLY GRAIL: LONG TERM CARE (LTC) INSURANCE

Long Term Care (LTC) Insurance is one of the best ways to pay for the Accidental Safari. A comprehensive LTC policy offers the rare dual benefits of personal choice and financial protection on this unavoidable and unpredictable journey. LTC Insurance guarantees a pool of money that the insured can draw from to pay for the types of care the policy covers, including in-home care, assisted living care, memory care, nursing care, respite care, and adult day care.

An additional point to consider when evaluating LTC Insurance is that reimbursement payments from the insurance company, although typically in the thousands of dollars per month, are not counted as income for income tax purposes.

FIGURING THE COST OF LONG TERM CARE INSURANCE

A Life Care Plan should include an analysis of the expected cost of long-term care and how these costs can be covered through LTC Insurance. Because the cost is heavily dependent on the insured's age and health at the time the policy is written, time is of the essence when buying the insurance.

The lower cost and longer coverage are two significant reasons to consider purchasing a policy when you are young and healthy. If you do not have LTC Insurance and experience a major medical event such as cancer or a heart attack, you generally become ineligible to purchase LTC Insurance and are uninsurable for a significant period of time following the event. If you had purchased LTC Insurance prior to the medical event, you would be covered throughout the event, regardless of your age at the time it occurred.

Fifteen years ago, my wife and I adopted two young children. Although we were healthy at the time, we decided to purchase LTC Insurance. If I had waited to apply for LTC Insurance, I would be paying significantly higher monthly premiums today due to my increased age. My client, Bea, also benefited from purchasing LTC Insurance when she was young.

THE EARLY BIRD GETS THE WORM

Bea was in her early sixties when she came to see me to review her estate plan. She was a planner, and her estate plan had been in place for many years. Among the documents I reviewed was her Long Term Care Insurance policy. As I reviewed the document, she complained that her monthly premium had recently increased from $121.00 per quarter to $151.00 per quarter. I noted that the policy would cover the costs of care at a maximum daily rate of $290.00 per day for ten years! Additionally, the daily rate of coverage would increase every year at a rate of five percent, which is more than the average annual inflation increase in the costs of long-term care! Bea was way ahead of the curve.

"You are paying $151.00 per quarter for this coverage? Most people are paying this amount and more per month for this type of coverage. You have a great policy! Bea, how old were you when you bought the policy?"

"I was twenty-nine," she replied.

"Twenty-nine? Who buys a Long Term Care policy at twenty-nine?" I asked, wondering if her family had a history of long-term care issues, like dementia.

She explained that when she was twenty-nine she was working for a company that brought in monthly motivational speakers. One of the speakers had explained how Long Term Care Insurance worked. She had liked the idea and bought a policy, one that will serve her well for the rest of her life. We should all be so lucky.

ADDITIONAL FACTORS AFFECTING LTC INSURANCE PREMIUMS

Other factors that affect the cost of LTC Insurance premiums are the maximum daily benefit rate (the maximum amount the policy will pay each day for your care) and the number of years of care the maximum daily rate would be paid. The maximum daily benefit rate times the number of years of coverage determines the lifetime maximum the policy will pay. So, a daily rate of $183.00 per day for 30 months would provide a total lifetime maximum benefit of $165,000. A typical policy allows you to take less than the daily rate per day to extend the period of coverage. In the above example, if you took less than the $183.00 per day the coverage (time period) would be extended until the total lifetime benefit of $165,000 was expended.

Another factor that affects the cost of premiums is whether the policy includes an inflation rider. A policy that pays $200.00 per day for three years would have a lifetime maximum amount calculated as follows: 365 days X 3 years (number of years of care) X $200.00 (maximum daily rate) = $219,000 total benefit. If the policy had an inflation rider (typically between 3 and 5 percent per year), there would be a resultant increase in the total benefit of the policy each year by the amount of increase. A simple 5% per year inflation rider would increase the $200.00 daily benefit to $210.00 per day after the first year and the lifetime maximum benefit amount would increase to $229,805. The inflation rate of 5%, equaling a $10.00 increase in the maximum daily benefit, would be applied each of the three years of coverage to keep up with the average annual increase in the cost of long-term care.

If the inflation rate is a compounded rate, the 5% increase would be applied each year to the entire amount of coverage of the previous year, including the previous year's increase. In the example above, the daily benefit ($210.00) after the second year would increase by $10.50 because the compounded 5% increase would be applied to the second year maximum daily benefit of $210.00, not the original maximum daily benefit of $200.00.

Although this increase may appear insignificant on its surface, let's compare the difference in coverage after paying premiums for a period of ten years. The maximum daily benefit rate after ten years of simple 5% interest increases from $200.00 per day to $300.00 per day, or from $6,000 to $9,000 per month. The maximum daily rate after 10 years of 5% compounded interest would be $325.78 per day, or $9,773.40 per month. In this example, the difference between simple interest and a compounded interest inflation rider after 10 years equates to $773.40 per month. The inflation rider is an important optional feature that can help the policy keep pace with inflation, but it is important to remember that the policy holder will pay a higher monthly premium for that benefit.

Additional options are available in an LTC policy that will also affect the cost of the monthly premiums. These options include a bed reservation (which would hold your bed in a nursing home or other facility if you have to move temporarily to the hospital) and a premium suspension (which will stop the billing of the monthly insurance premiums once you have initiated a claim for benefits and begin to receive reimbursement from the policy for the costs of care).

THE COST VS. BENEFITS OF LTC INSURANCE

I always ask my clients during the initial consultation if they have LTC Insurance. Their answer is almost always "no," since fewer than ten percent of Americans have purchased LTC Insurance. When I ask "Why not?" the customary response is "Because it costs too much."

"How much would it cost for someone your age?"

"I don't know, but it would be expensive."

Expensive is a relative term. Adding monthly insurance premiums of $140.00 per month to an already tight budget may seem impossible to someone with no experience with an Accidental Safari. But to anyone who has witnessed a parent spending down their life savings during years of care, $140.00 a month, for insurance that would have covered the cost of that care, will look like a bargain.

I recommend that you get a quote for the costs of LTC Insurance from two or three insurance companies. When comparing policies, be sure that each company is providing a premium quote for policies that have equal benefits. Every buyer wants a policy with the greatest benefits and the lowest premiums, so shop around.

Two healthy 60-year-olds will pay an average of $3,335 a year for policies that will pay $340,000 in benefits. When you add the cost of a long-term care policy to the costs of Medicare Part B, a Medicare supplement plan, and drug coverage, a retired couple could easily be looking at $700 to $800 per month in insurance costs.

(https://www.consumerreports.org/cro/2012/08/long-term-care-insurance/index.htm)[11]

WHAT ABOUT RISING LTC INSURANCE PREMIUMS?

Ideally, LTC Insurance premiums would remain the same over time, but that has not been the case with most policies. In the face of steady increases in care costs, and the fact that people are living longer and accepting professional care earlier in the journey, most insurance companies have had to raise the premiums for LTC policy owners. If you have a policy and have not yet had an increase in the premium, it will likely come sometime in the near future.

An increase in LTC Insurance premiums leaves you with three options: pay the increase, take a reduction in benefits to waive the premium increase, or drop the policy altogether.

Dropping the policy should be the last resort. Remember that the cost of the policy is primarily based on your age. None of us is getting any younger. If you own a policy today and are considering dropping the policy, check to see what the premium costs would be for a new policy, at your current age, with the same benefits as your current policy. You will probably realize that you actually have a bargain with the original policy.

To determine if your LTC policy adequately addresses the current costs of care, compare the current maximum daily benefit of your policy with the current daily costs of care in your area. Also compare home care costs, assisted living costs, and nursing care costs. If the benefit covers a majority of the costs or enough so that the payment of the monthly care costs would be sustainable without depleting all of your savings and investments, you should keep the policy. The purpose of the LTC policy is to protect your assets by reducing the risk that you will have to spend down all of your assets to pay for care, while expanding your care options and giving you peace of mind.

The local cost of care at different kinds of facilities in your area can be found at https://www.genworth.com/about-us/industry-expertise/cost-of-care.html or you can search the internet for "Genworth compare long-term care costs."

The decision whether to keep the policy, reduce the benefits, or drop the policy altogether must take into consideration several variables: your income, total assets, current health, family health history, care expectations from family, overall care plan, eligibility for other resources, sustainability, etc. This decision is another fork in the road on the Safari where the advice of a competent guide is a must.

Another issue to consider in purchasing or keeping LTC Insurance is the financial viability of the insurance company. Ten of the top twenty insurance companies in LTC Insurance sales have stopped selling LTC Insurance in the last 10 years.

Since you may not use the insurance for 20 to 30 years, you want an insurance policy that is backed by a company with staying power. A company that has been around for a long time with a good financial rating is more likely to be there when you need it. Fortunately, the payment of benefits from LTC policies sold by companies that have exited the business has continued to be covered by either the issuing company or other companies that have purchased the policies. The insurance industry has stood behind those companies that have defaulted on claims.

A common complaint of potential purchasers of LTC Insurance has been, "I could pay monthly premiums for years and, if I die suddenly one day, I will have wasted all that money." Interestingly, people do not have the same complaints about car insurance or fire insurance. No one goes to bed at night disappointed that they did not get to make a claim on their car insurance that day. Knowing that our homes and cars are protected gives us peace of mind. Why, then, are we resistant to pay for insurance that will cover our care when we can no longer care for ourselves or our loved one?

LTC INSURANCE POLICY OPTIONS

As the gray tsunami of Baby Boomers advances toward long-term care, insurance companies are getting more creative. The federal government is also responding by not taxing LTC Insurance policies that cover the cost of long-term care.

To counter the issue of buyers' resistance to buying an insurance policy they never want to use, the insurance industry has developed a hybrid LTC policy. The hybrid policy has both a life insurance and a Long Term Care Insurance component within a single policy. If the insured dies suddenly, the policy beneficiary will receive the proceeds of the life insurance. If the insured needs long-term care, the policy benefit will be spent down to cover the cost of care. The insured is guaranteed a return from the policy, whether in life or through death.

A hybrid policy is typically paid by a single premium and not by monthly payments like traditional insurance, which means there are no monthly premiums that could be subject to rate increases. With current savings and CD rates low, it might make sense, for those who can afford it, to leverage a premium amount and park a lump sum of cash in a hybrid LTC policy.

Another option for couples to pay for care is a joint hybrid contract (JHC). A JHC consists of a "second-to-die" life insurance policy and a LTC Insurance policy for both of the insureds. Since the life insurance component does not pay out until the second spouse dies, a couple might qualify for this policy, including the LTC Insurance part, even if one spouse has marginal health. Some companies allow applicants to qualify for this insurance through a phone interview only (a simplified issue), which may or may not include a health record review or medical exam.

An example of a Joint Hybrid Contract (JHC) might look like this: A married couple ages 68 and 67 might expect to pay a single $100,000.00 premium for a JHC second-to-die life insurance policy that would pay $140,000.00 to the named beneficiary at the death of the second spouse and would carry an LTC Insurance maximum benefit of $2,800.00 per month for each spouse for their lifetimes. As the LTC benefit was paid out, the life insurance component would be reduced. After $140,000.00 in LTC benefits were paid out, there would be no residual life insurance benefit, but the LTC coverage would continue to be paid for the policyholders' lifetimes. One should consider, however, that $2,800.00 per month will not go very far toward the total monthly costs of a nursing home in the current environment, and even less so in another ten or twenty years.

Another twist allowed for LTC Insurance plans is the ability to roll an old life insurance policy or annuity policy that has a cash value into a new policy with an LTC benefit, without having to pay income tax on the growth in the old policy.

BUILDING THE PARACHUTE AFTER THE JUMP

Because the focus of my law practice is elder law, the vast majority of my clients are between 60 and 90 years of age. I see clients who have had the forethought to develop a Life Care Plan in advance, but I also see many clients whose default plan is to step out "into thin air." I would describe this approach to life as "Ready, Fire, Aim!" Have you known people like that? There is actually a fine line between "people of action" and people who "act first and ask questions later."

Sadly, many people discover their need for an LTC Insurance parachute only after they have jumped, or been thrown, from the plane.

WHEN THE SAFARI COMES AND YOU'RE LIVING MONTH TO MONTH

Mildred came to see me because she would not be able to make the next month's mortgage payment. She and her husband, Don, were old enough to be retired, but financial woes had forced them to continue working to supplement their retirement. They were living month to month. One day, Mildred found that their lives had changed in a moment. Don was in the intensive care unit at the hospital, unresponsive, and in an induced coma to reduce brain swelling.

Don's pension was automatically deposited into his account, and every month Don had faithfully written a check to cover the mortgage. But Don would not be able to write the check next month and, because Mildred's name was not on the account, she wouldn't be able to write the check either. Mildred came to see me to ask how she could make the house payment on the first of the month. Mildred and Don woke up on the Serengeti without a plan; not even a sleeping bag.

Lack of planning (or a parachute) and Don's health emergency put them both in an extremely precarious position. If Don had given Mildred a Power of Attorney to act for him in financial matters, she could have gained immediate access to the account and paid the mortgage. The only remedy for Don and Mildred at this point was a guardianship for Don, which might allow her to get an order from a court authorizing her to access the account, a time-consuming and costly option.

What do you do if you find yourself suddenly having to build a parachute on the way down? Go back to the basics.

First, an experienced guide is essential to your survival. Find an elder law attorney who will help you develop an emergency plan of action. The National Association of Elder Law Attorneys (https://www.naela.org), a national association of Geriatric Care Managers (http://www.aginglifecare.org), or the local Council on Aging are all good places to find experienced guides in your area.

Second, find an individual or a team of individuals who will take the Safari with you and advocate for you.

Third, your advocate(s) must be authorized (through appropriate legal documentation) to act on your behalf in all medical and financial matters.

Fourth, the advocate(s) will need to be directed and equipped.

Finally, your guide will provide you and your advocate(s) with vital advice concerning health, housing, finance, and legal matters. Your guide will give you a realistic overview of the available options and help you identify the likely direction or level of care you will need in the future. For example, if additional care is needed at home, or if you cannot go home, a care facility that meets your needs will be selected.

All of these decisions raise financial considerations. An elder law attorney or geriatric care manager is the most likely person to guide you through the process of identifying all of the available sources of funds to pay for your care, including veteran's benefits and Medicaid. Given the level of care that is needed and your financial situation, payment will likely come from your own financial resources, Long Term Care Insurance, or from other resources for which you may be eligible. Fortunately, Medicaid exists to serve as a safety net for people who cannot pay for the cost of care. Information about Medicaid can be found in **Chapter 8: The Ultimate Safety Net.**

7

TAKING THE FIRST STEPS

I recommend that everyone create a Life Care Plan in the event they suddenly find themselves on an Accidental Safari. Enjoying peace of mind prior to and during the early days of the Safari frequently depends on the planning and preparation that we have done. The first step in the process involves an evaluation of your net worth, income, and life style. Our goal is to find a balance between what you have, what you need, and what you want.

What you have includes your income, your principal assets, and other resources available to you. What you need deals with your overall cost of living compared to the essentials of life. What you want involves those things to be acquired or participated in, both tangible and intangible.

Peace of mind can come when you know that what you have is sufficient to supply the things that you and your loved ones may need. However, ultimately we do not have control of our health or life, and real peace must come from outside of ourselves.

> "I'm not saying this because I need anything. I have learned to be content no matter what happens to me. (NIRV)"
>
> — Philippians 4:11

As I work with my clients, I listen to their goals and ask their opinions. We work together to develop a plan that addresses the essential issues of health, housing, finance, law, and leisure. We consider the ways taxes can be minimized or avoided. We consider the issue of family legacy; provisions for the disabled, wayward, addicted, or mentally ill beneficiaries; and the costs of long-term healthcare and the financial sustainability of that care. Finances are important, but they are only a piece of the puzzle.

ASSESS YOUR ASSETS

When meeting with clients to develop a Life Care Plan, the focus will turn to the sustainability of the plan if the need for long-term care becomes a primary issue. It is helpful, therefore, to examine all the pieces of the Life Care Plan with the clients. They may be fearful of having to pinch pennies in the event one of them ends up on an Accidental Safari. They want to know that they have enough assets to cover the risk. If I can tell them, "in a worst-case scenario, with your current level of income and savings, you would be able to cover the costs of long-term care for many years," then I have given them a world of relief.

These discussions provide peace of mind as clients come to understand how the assets they have can be allocated to not only cover risks but to achieve goals such as leisure and philanthropy. Peace and security do not come solely from having money in the bank, and money cannot purchase the things that are the most precious.

Assessing your assets also requires that you clearly understand the terms and conditions of those assets. The experience of my client, Charlene, illustrates what I mean.

THE FINE PRINT

Charlene came to see me after her husband died. She brought a letter from their insurance company that read: "Dear Mrs. Rogers, Please accept our condolences on the passing of Mr. Rogers. Enclosed is a claim form. Please complete the claim form and return it with a certified death certificate, and we will forward you the proceeds of the life insurance policy: thirty-nine thousand five hundred and forty-seven dollars ($39,547.00, plus interest."

Charlene also pulled out what appeared to be an old, tightly folded insurance policy. I could read the large print at the top of the page from across the table. It read "$100,000 Life Insurance Policy." When she saw that my eyes fell on the bold title she said, "I don't understand."

I read through the policy and pointed out the language that said the policy benefit, unfortunately for Charlene, would actually lose value as the insured advanced in age. She sat very still, trying to understand the meaning of my words.

"Mr. Tizzano," she finally said, barely above a whisper, "I didn't know that this was that kind of policy, and I'm pretty sure that my husband didn't know that it was that kind of policy."

It's not uncommon for people to have a distorted view, or no view at all, of their financial health, to misunderstand how certain investments work. So one of the first steps toward developing a Life Care Plan is understanding your assets. Acquiring this understanding may require some effort on your part.

Because my law practice focuses on estate planning, I do not offer financial planning advice. I do not give assessments of investment portfolios, perform risk/return analysis on investments, or forecast investment outcomes. These are, however, important steps to include in a financial planning review. I recommend, therefore, that you have all of your finances reviewed every few years, at a minimum by an investment advisor. You should have them reviewed more frequently if you are the kind of person who does not read the monthly statements (or even open the envelopes).

Most people have their assets in multiple places, so even if you have an investment advisor, you probably have additional investments or savings accounts in other places. If you don't keep "all your eggs in one basket," it is, therefore, not only helpful, but necessary to have a periodic confessional with an investment advisor in which you discuss your total financial picture. This detailed discussion will allow you to reacquaint yourself with what you have and how it's working for you.

You should also conduct a performance evaluation of your investment advisor from time to time. It is prudent to have someone other than your advisor perform the assessment. If you do not have a financial advisor and you have savings in excess of an emergency fund, you should hire a financial professional or qualified friend to review your assets with you. If you are looking for an investment advisor, you might ask someone you trust or whom you know to be financially responsible for a referral to a financial advisor. Remember, though, that peace of mind isn't only about assets, as the following two stories illustrate:

MONEY ISN'T EVERYTHING

Mickey and Fran came to see me about preparing an estate plan. They have an adult child who is disabled and living at home. I suggested they prepare an estate plan that would include a special needs trust for the disabled child. The trust assets would provide a financial safety net after Mickey and Fran were gone while protecting their child's eligibility for Social Security and Medicaid benefits.

Mickey talked about his job with a certain bread company. He has driven the same delivery route for more than 35 years. Although he is eligible for retirement, he said he didn't think he would retire. He loves his work. I asked him what his retirement pay would be, and he said he didn't know for sure. I explained that he could probably get a dramatic raise in pay if he were to retire from his current job and seek employment with another business that had a similar delivery system.

Mickey and Fran agreed to gather the information we'd need to prepare their estate plan, and we made an appointment to meet again in a few weeks.

In our society, work is usually an exchange of time for money. We give a day of our lives in exchange for a quantity of dollars. Since we have exchanged our days for dollars, dollars have value, and the things we buy with those dollars are valuable, too. But can peace of mind, forgiveness, health, love, and friendship be purchased with dollars? Of course not. Ultimately, the things that matter most in life cannot be purchased.

Mickey and Fran returned to my office. I was anxious to ask what he had found out about his retirement benefits and how he and Fran were leaning with regard to the whole retirement idea. Mickey said that he completely understood about piling up income from a new job after retiring from his current job. He was smiling, though, as he told me again that he loved his job and had decided to stay put. He enjoys his visits with customers every day as he works his route. He couldn't walk away from that. He was content. He was at peace.

Contentment is a gift. Mickey is content, and the exercise we went through together has made him appreciate his work all the more. It's as if he retired and gets to do exactly what he wants to do, which is exactly the thing he is already doing. He is a fortunate man, indeed.

WHEN IS ENOUGH, ENOUGH?

Gladys was a stereotypical "little old lady." She would come to see me every couple of years to "tweak" her estate plan. She came into one meeting with a big smile on her face. She pulled a letter out of her purse and sat waving the envelope at me and explaining how she had won a lot of money and what she was going to do with it. She told me she was going to pay off her granddaughter's student loan, buy her grandson a car, and take the entire family on a cruise.

She was there to ask me to help her collect her winnings from the Sports Illustrated Sweepstakes. Upon close inspection, however, although the letter appeared to say that she had won a million dollars, I pointed out the very small print that clarified that she "may" be a winner. This revelation hit her hard after days of excitement and she broke down in my office and cried. She explained that what made the situation most unbearable was that now she couldn't do all those nice things for her family.

Gladys had lived through the Great Depression of the 1930's. As a result of her childhood experiences, she had become a hard worker and a hard saver. She had seen her family and the entire country in a state of desperate need, and she never wanted to experience that again. Sadly, she was never able to master her fear of not having enough.

When she composed herself again, I leaned across the table and tried to explain that I thought her ideas were great ways to bless her family. I reminded her that she had more than 2 million dollars in her financial accounts and if paying off her granddaughter's student loan, buying her grandson a car, and taking the family on a cruise were important to her, she could still do those things.

With wide eyes she looked at me and slowly shook her head. "Oh no," she said, "I couldn't do that."

The saddest part of this story is that she really could have done it, without jeopardizing her financial security at all. But she just couldn't determine what "enough" was.

Your income, after retirement, is all the money that continues to come to you each month after you have stopped showing up for work. Income includes checks in the mailbox, automatic deposits, and dividends and interest from investment growth. Income can include disability payments, Social Security payments, pensions, rental income, royalties, etc. It's everything that comes in on a recurring basis.

Your principal assets are assets that you have under your direct control. These assets include savings accounts, investment accounts, retirement accounts, rental property, and even the equity in your home if you are using a reverse mortgage. All of these items can be income-producing assets. But there are additional types of assets that do not generate income. Non-income producing assets may include your home, other real (non-rental) property, personal property, checking accounts, insurance policies, cars, boats, planes, recreational vehicles, and timeshares. These non-income producing assets are either appreciating or depreciating assets.

Other resources include benefits that are available or might be available if they are applied for. They include public and private sources of funding and services for food and shelter through food stamps and vouchers. "Meals on Wheels" or other nonprofit food services are available through senior centers and/or local churches. Many benefits are available to veterans such as payments for service-related and non-service-related disabilities or for in-home aide services. Health services are also available through Medicare and can include payments for hospital and physician services as well as home health and hospice services. You will recall that Medicaid is a federal program that pays for long-term care when the patient's health issues cease to be "medical" and become issues of "care." Many non-profit charities such as Catholic Community Services and Lutheran Community Services offer low-cost services to the elderly or the disabled and can arrange volunteer assistance for home repairs, volunteer companions, or a home aide.

Understanding your income and principal assets, and any additional resources available to you, will give you a clear picture of what you have to work with as you begin to consider both your needs and wants. Of course, your perspective will depend in part on whether you or your loved one have actually begun an Accidental Safari or if you are merely preparing for the possibility of one. If you are preparing for a potential Safari, you will have minimized the "Accidental" component. A Safari could still sneak up on you, but your emergency kit will be packed and ready.

KNOW YOUR NEEDS

Your needs consist of the regular monthly expenses of living, including food and shelter. These expenses vary greatly depending on whether your home is fully paid for and whether an Accidental Safari has begun. If the Safari has begun, you will need to factor the actual costs of care into your needs analysis.

Take a look at your current monthly budget. You can begin to play around with the data to evaluate different scenarios. Some individuals know their monthly expenses to the penny, while others have no idea. If you have little or no idea what you are actually spending each month, you should begin to keep track of your expenses for a few months. Make note of every dollar of income that comes in and document every outgoing dollar. Is the income completely spent by the end of the month or is there a little residual income left over? If it's completely gone, and you have had to take a little from your savings (or some other source) every month to make ends meet, what is the average amount of money that is required to supplement your monthly income?

What if your monthly expenses suddenly increased dramatically to cover the cost of care at home or in an assisted living, memory care, or nursing facility? What current expenses would go away completely or decrease? Would you be able to sell your home and downsize?

If you are already on an Accidental Safari, these questions are important to consider because decisions will need to be made quickly. If you are simply planning for the future, you will have more time to evaluate the issues and begin taking steps to address them.

While it is sometimes easy to see the red flags waving at the people around us, our tendency may be to ignore the warning lights in our own situation and slip into denial. We can rationalize our way around the circumstances or deny their seriousness, but it is far wiser in the long run if we face the potential dangers before we reach a point of no return. Unfortunately, as the Safari ramps up, many of the best options will have already been passed by.

The difference between planning for a potential Safari and being abducted and forced into one can be described as the difference between a doctor's office and the emergency room.

In the emergency room, you are literally fighting for your life. Things happen very quickly. "Get the heart beating! Get the breathing started! Stop the bleeding!" It's really a life-and-death situation. In the doctor's office, we talk about weight loss, exercise, cholesterol levels, and preventative treatment. Things happen very slowly. We often take the long-term approach in order to avoid the emergency room.

If you are planning ahead and preparing for a potential Safari, although the numbers may be somewhat fluid, you can get a fairly accurate picture of the impact. You can determine if your income, assets, and other resources will be enough to cover your expenses as well as your wants, which may include cross-country trips in the RV to visit the grandkids or your personal "bucket list."

WEIGH YOUR WANTS

So how much is enough? Once you have considered the consequences of a potential Safari, you have a basis for determining the amount of time and resources you can put into pursuing your wants. I enjoy challenging my clients to consider what is next, what is yet undone!

In an earlier story, Gladys had 2.5 million dollars, a mortgage-free home, and a very generous monthly income. Her financial safety net was deep enough to pay off her granddaughter's college loans, buy a car for her grandson, and enjoy a cruise with her family. Sadly, she did not trust in the sufficiency of her safety net and couldn't make the move from fear to joy.

Fear is a motivating factor. For Gladys, fear motivated her to hoard her money and she sacrificed the joy and satisfaction she would have received in blessing her family. You can use fear and insecurity positively or negatively. Use it as a motivation to assess your true financial picture, evaluate real potential future risks, and then take steps to address and overcome the fear. If that realistic assessment indicates significant shortfalls in health or finances, take steps to understand and address the shortfall.

There is only so much you can do or should do in planning for the Safari. That effort is different for everyone. Do not be frozen by the fear that the costs of long-term care will destroy your financial security. If your long-term care risk is not covered by LTC Insurance, you will likely be responsible for the costs of your care. For some seniors, veteran's benefits will supplement some of the care costs. And finally, when people cannot pay for their care, Medicaid kicks in as the ultimate safety net.

Of course the "ultimate safety net" is not the money in the bank or Medicaid or even our own health. Our hope must transcend the material, it must be bigger than who we are and what we have. If the circumstances get bigger than I can handle, and they could at any moment, my hope is in my God who loves me and does all things well.

8

THE ULTIMATE SAFETY NET

At this point you may be wondering, "If I am, or can become, eligible for Medicaid to pay for my care, why wouldn't I do that?" In response, I must acknowledge that there are widely different views concerning government responsibility and personal responsibility with regard to the payment of long-term care costs. Another question that I'm frequently asked is, "How can a lawyer ethically walk people around the system and make the government pay for those who could (and should) pay for their own care?"

I address both of these questions by first asking a question of my own.

"Is it unethical for an attorney to inform a client about Medicaid rules?" This is not a new question. In 1997, in a move to avoid placing blame for the rising costs of long-term nursing care on government, Congress adopted a punitive measure referred to as the "Granny's Lawyer Goes to Jail" law.

In essence, the law decreed that anyone who charged a fee for advising seniors on ways to plan for government assistance with long-term care costs risked committing a federal crime.

That was a bit unsettling to say the least. Fortunately, the United States Supreme Court determined that Congress could not prohibit an attorney from advising a client about the law and deemed the "Granny's Lawyer Goes to Jail" law to be unconstitutional.

Personally, I am a fiscal conservative. As such, I expect that the government will be responsible with my hard-earned tax dollars. Furthermore, since I have contributed money into the Medicare/Medicaid program from every paycheck I have ever earned, I have a right to expect that the program will be there to help me if and when I need it, by doing exactly what I was told it would do: provide me with medical and long-term care coverage if I need it.

I do not help my clients "beat" or "take advantage of" the system. I tell them how the system works. The system has safeguards in place that protect the government. These safeguards prevent people from gifting their money away in order to become financially eligible for Medicaid. The system also has safeguards that protect a well spouse from becoming financially destitute in order to qualify the ill spouse for Medicaid. My experience shows that most people will choose to use government benefits to pay for their care if they can become eligible, but not everyone chooses the government safety net.

Medicare vs. Medicaid

REMINDER: Medicare covers medical care costs for people over the age of 65. At the point in time when the patient's "medical" issue is reclassified as a "care" issue, medical insurance coverage and Medicare will end.

This is where the Accidental Safari and long-term care begin. If the expenses of long-term care are not paid by LTC Insurance, the costs must be paid out of pocket (through private pay), through Medicaid, or through veteran's disability benefits or some combination of these resources.

TO QUALIFY OR NOT TO QUALIFY? THAT IS THE QUESTION!

I am frequently asked if Medicaid will take assets from applicants who have assets above the allowed amount. Medicaid does not *take* assets to pay for care, but Medicaid will not *pay* for your care if you are not financially eligible to receive Medicaid benefits. This means that you will have to pay for care out of the assets that you own that have made you ineligible. This process is called a "spend down."

If you are faced with the choice to pay privately for long-term care, resulting in the "spend down" of your assets, or to take steps to become Medicaid-eligible, you should consider the following:

If you require care but have too much money to qualify for Medicaid, you can pay for your care out of pocket and ultimately spend down your assets to the point at which you would financially qualify for Medicaid.

If you are married, you can become Medicaid-qualified by legally transferring your assets to your (well) spouse in a manner allowed by the Medicaid rules.

If you are single, your primary option will be the spend down scenario explained above.

Let's evaluate Peg and Ernie's situation:

PRESERVING ASSETS
THROUGH ANNUITIES

Peg came to see me to ask about Medicaid for her husband, Ernie, who had recently become a resident of a local nursing home. She told me their story, and I explained how Medicaid could work for them.

For Ernie to qualify for Medicaid, he would need to meet both physical and financial qualifications. Qualifying physically meant that he needed assistance with at least three of the activities of daily living (i.e. dressing, bathing, toileting, transferring, eating), or have a cognitive impairment such that assistance is necessary for his safety and well-being.

To qualify financially, Ernie could not own more than $2,000 in assets. Therefore, all of their jointly owned property would need to be transferred to Peg, as the well spouse. The transfer of assets between spouses for Medicaid eligibility does not create a period of ineligibility and is not a taxable transfer. It is also not subject to the 5-year "look-back period" for Medicaid eligibility purposes.

As the well spouse in Washington State, Peg may own the following:

- A home of any value
- A vehicle of any value
- Life insurance up to $1,500 in face value
- Burial plots and pre-paid funerals for both spouses
- Personal property of any value
- Cash or assets in savings and investment accounts of $54,726 or $120,900 (depending on how long the Medicaid recipient has been in care and whether he/she has paid privately for care during that period). These assets are referred to as the "Community Spouse Resource Allowance" or "CSRA."

Ernie and Peg had been married for more than 60 years and raised five children together. He had been in the nursing home for four months. His monthly income was $2,200, and her monthly income was $800.

The costs of Ernie's care ($9,600), and Peg's living expenses ($2,400), totaling $12,000 per month, were paid out of their monthly income ($3,000) and from savings and investments ($9,000). The remaining balance of the couple's savings and investment accounts was approximately $400,000 after the last monthly expense payments.

Under the current scenario, the plan would be sustainable for approximately 44 months ($400,000 in savings and investments divided by a $9,000 monthly shortfall equals 44 months).

I explained to Peg that if she did not take the steps to qualify Ernie for Medicaid, she would deplete her assets in 44 months.

To qualify for Medicaid, Ernie could own a maximum of $2,000. Therefore, the only asset that could be held in both Peg and Ernie's names would be the joint checking account if it received only Ernie's monthly retirement income. Peg's income would have to be redirected to a new account that would be in her name only.

Although most couples will have all of their monthly income payments deposited into a joint checking account, in cases where one spouse is receiving Medicaid benefits, only the income/pension to the Medicaid recipient should continue to be deposited into the joint account. Income payments to the well spouse should be directed into a separate account set up in the name of the well spouse only. The well spouse should contact Social Security to direct the change in the deposit of the Social Security payment of the well spouse to the new account. DO NOT DISCUSS, OR MAKE CHANGES TO, THE SOCIAL SECURITY INCOME DEPOSIT OF THE MEDICAID APPLICANT/RECIPIENT TO THE JOINT CHECKING ACCOUNT WHEN SPEAKING WITH THE SOCIAL SECURITY ADMINISTRATION.

When making adjustments to direct deposits and to checking accounts, DO NOT CHANGE THE ACCOUNT OF THE MEDICAID APPLICANT/RECIPIENT IN ANY WAY. The names of both spouses must remain on the original checking account although that account will receive only the Medicaid recipient's retirement and Social Security income. If you do not follow this advice and discuss the Medicaid recipient's direct deposit with Social Security, they will likely ask to speak with him/her. If dementia or competency issues are suspected, Social Security will stop the payments and will require the well spouse to become the Medicaid recipient's "Designated Payee." This is an additional and unnecessary hassle that can be completely avoided.

You may be thinking, "Wait a minute. Ernie's retirement is $2,200 each month, so he is over the $2,000 he is allowed to have as soon as his pension hits the account." But here is how it actually works if Ernie is on Medicaid:

The Medicaid recipient cannot end the month with more than $2,000 in his or her checking account. If Ernie ended the previous month with $500 in his checking account, the new month opens with a $2,200 deposit. Ernie would now have $2,700 in his account.

The nursing home would send him a bill for $9,600 for the cost of care. Medicaid would also send a letter to Ernie confirming that Ernie is qualified for Medicaid for the current month and stating that his participation amount is $2,200. A $2,200 check would be sent from Ernie's checking account along with a copy of the Medicaid qualifying letter to the nursing home. The nursing home would then bill Medicaid for the difference.

Ernie and Peg would then have just $500 in the joint checking account, which is different from Peg's checking account.

Remember the Medicaid rules stipulate that Ernie can have no more than $2,000 in his name. I told Peg that she would need to put all of the couple's other assets in her name alone in separate accounts. I could tell from Peg's body language and the look on her face that she was uncomfortable with the idea of transferring their assets to herself individually. Her silence allowed me to continue.

"Your home will need to be transferred from both of your names into your name, Peg." I said.

"How do I do that?" she asked.

"It requires that you and Ernie execute a deed transferring the house to you. Can Ernie sign his name, or do you have power of attorney for him?"

"He can sign," she replied.

I continued to explain how Medicaid works. In addition, Peg could own a vehicle of any value, a small life insurance policy with up to $1,500 in face value, burial plots and pre-paid funerals for both spouses, and personal property of any value. The amount of cash, or funds in bank accounts and investments is called "Community Spouse Resource Allowance." Because Ernie had already been in the nursing home for more than 30 days, the CSRA allowance for Peg (the well spouse) would be $120,900.

I told Peg the bad news. "You have $400,000 in investment assets, but the CSRA allowance is $120,900." That meant that Peg had an excess of $279,100 ($400,000 less the $120,900 allowance limit) of assets over the amount that she could own if Ernie was to qualify for Medicaid.

Then I told Peg the good news. The Medicaid rules allow all of the excess assets, the nearly $280,000 in Peg's case, to be converted to income. Peg, as the well spouse, could keep all of the income earned in her name. That meant that the approximately $280,000 would not be included in the couple's financial picture that the Medicaid worker would use to calculate Ernie's eligibility for Medicaid.

To qualify Ernie for Medicaid, Peg would need to purchase an annuity in the amount of approximately

$290,000, the amount exceeding the CSRA allowance. (To recap, Peg and Ernie owned $400,000 in savings and investments. They needed to reduce their assets by the amount over the CSRA limit, $290,000. Purchasing a $290,000 Medicaid-qualified annuity would provide income to Peg, and would leave $110,000 in Peg's separate account, which would be under the CSRA asset limit.) When Peg buys the annuity, the state (Washington, in Peg's case) would be named as the residual beneficiary of the annuity. The annuity would generate 60 equal monthly payments (spanning five years) to Peg of approximately $4,830. Under Medicaid rules, Peg could keep all the income generated in her name, including the annuity payments and any other income she may receive such as a pension or Social Security income.

If Peg were to die at the end of year one, she would have received approximately $58,000 in annuity payments ($4,830 x 12 monthly payments). Medicaid would have paid out approximately $60,000 for Ernie's care during year one. (Ernie contributed $2,200 of his income per month and, although Ernie's monthly nursing home bill was $9,600 per month under private pay, Medicaid pays the nursing home at a reduced rate. For purposes of this example, we will assume that Medicaid pays $60,000 annually to the nursing home for Ernie's care.)

If Peg purchased a $290,000 annuity, after receiving $58,000 in income from the annuity during year one, $232,000 would remain in the annuity at the end of the first year. If Peg died suddenly at the end of year one, Medicaid would be reimbursed from the annuity for the $60,000 in benefits paid for Ernie's care in year one, and Peg and Ernie's beneficiaries would receive the $172,000 residual value of the annuity.

If Peg died at the end of year four and Ernie is still in the nursing home, Peg would have received four years of monthly annuity payments (at a rate of $58,000 annually) for a total of $232,000 in income payments. Medicaid payments for Ernie's nursing home care for four years would have totaled $260,000. The state would recover the $58,000 residual value in the annuity as reimbursement, and there would be no residual benefit for Peg and Ernie's beneficiaries.

An annuity is an investment that pays back your investment with interest over time through monthly payments. It is considered a conservative investment. The risk of loss is low, because it is insured, but the return is also low.

Technically, at Ernie's death, the state could also recover from any assets that Ernie owned at his death, but since everything had been legally transferred to Peg before he became Medicaid-qualified, the state would have no basis for claiming any assets from Peg's estate because she did not receive Medicaid benefits.

The assets owned in Peg's name at her death would pass to the beneficiaries named in her estate planning documents or the designated beneficiaries of her individual investment accounts.

I covered all of this information with Peg and then summarized. "So, your current monthly expenses are approximately $9,600 for Ernie and $2,400 for you. This totals $12,000 per month, which is being paid from your joint income, savings, and investments. Right now, you have $400,000 remaining in savings and investment accounts, which gives you about four years of reserve.

Peg nodded her head and said that she didn't think that they would "want to get Ernie on Medicaid." She said that they would be okay; that was what they had saved for, "to take care of each other when the time came."

I assured her that while I understood and admired her resolve, in a year their assets would be down to about $285,000. "If that concerns you, you could always take action at that time. And in two and a half years, Ernie would be eligible for Medicaid because the assets would be below the $120,900 CSRA allowance. You would not need to move any assets into an annuity then, but you would need to apply. I could help you to apply then if you wished."

If Ernie survived the depletion of all their savings, Peg's options would be to take Ernie home, try to borrow money to pay for his care, or apply for Medicaid. The nursing home would not make Ernie leave, but the bill would have to be paid. Medicaid is the safety net when the recipient is destitute.

Peg could have used the Medicaid-qualified annuity to qualify Ernie for Medicaid sooner. The goal of public policy is not to require the well spouse to become destitute and end up needing government assistance, too.

Remember: excess assets, above the CSRA limit, can be converted to income through the purchase of a Medicaid-qualified annuity by the well spouse. For an annuity to be approved for Medicaid purposes, it must meet the following criteria:

1.   It must be irrevocable and nontransferable.

2.   It must be amortized over at least five years (60 months), or it can be less if the life expectancy of the well spouse is less than 60 months. This means that the annuity amount will be distributed back to the well spouse in 60 equal monthly payments.

3.   The state must be the named residual beneficiary of the annuity if the well spouse dies within the 5-year payout period. The state would receive an amount up to the total value of all the benefits the Medicaid recipient received up to the date of death of the well spouse.

A few alternative scenarios for Peg and Ernie's story can give a broader understanding of how Medicaid might be applied. Let's assume the basic facts of Peg and Ernie's situation remain the same.

INVESTMENT ASSETS UNDER THE CSRA ALLOWANCE

Ernie's monthly income is $2,200 and Peg's monthly income is $800. His monthly cost of care is about $9,600, and her living expenses are about $2,400, totaling $12,000 per month. Expenses are covered by income, their savings, and investments.

Changing the amount of Peg and Ernie's savings and investments changes the picture significantly. Instead of $400,000 in savings and investments, let's assume that Peg and Ernie have just $40,000. At their current spending rate of $9,000 per month, their nest egg of $40,000 would last less than four months. Something would need to be done quickly.

Because the assets on hand are less than the Medicaid benchmarks (CSRA of $53,000 or $120,900), Peg would not need to shelter assets in a Medicaid-qualified annuity.

Ernie would be financially eligible for Medicaid immediately. Peg would only need to prepare and submit a Medicaid application.

Never submit an application for Medicaid unless the applicant is financially eligible because excess assets will create a period of ineligibility.

MINIMUM MONTHLY INCOME OF $2,000 FOR THE WELL SPOUSE

Medicaid rules provide that Peg (the well spouse) should receive a minimum monthly income of $2,000 per month. In the above example, Peg and Ernie have only $40,000 in assets, and Peg's total income is $800 in Social Security income. Peg is $1,200 per month short of the $2,000 that Medicaid deems a minimum monthly income amount for the well spouse. Therefore, instead of Ernie contributing all of his retirement income ($2,200) to the nursing facility, his share of the cost of care would be reduced by $1,200 per month. He would pay $1,000 of his retirement income to the nursing home, and the residual $1,200 would be left in the joint checking account to be available to Peg as her minimum monthly needs allowance. The $1,200 would be added to Peg's $800 monthly Social Security income, bringing her to the $2,000 minimum monthly income amount that Medicaid deems Peg is entitled to.

FINANCIAL INELIGIBILITY DUE
TO IRA ASSETS

Peg and Ernie's actual financial picture consisted of $400,000 in cash, savings, and investments. These assets would be transferred to Peg individually, as the well spouse. She would keep up to the $120,000 maximum allowance in cash, savings, and investments and shelter the remainder through the purchase of a Medicaid-qualified annuity.

In an alternative scenario, imagine that the $400,000 resides in Ernie's Individual Retirement Account (IRA). Preserving that nest egg will still require transfer of the assets to Peg, as the well spouse, and she will be able to keep a predetermined amount and be required to shelter the rest.

In this case, the first step will still be to transfer the assets. If the asset is Ernie's IRA, transferring Ernie's IRA to Peg would trigger a payout of all of Ernie's tax-qualified IRA, creating an income tax obligation on the $400,000. The tax would be approximately $150,000.

Peg and Ernie will need to decide whether it is prudent to transfer the funds and pay the taxes, leaving Peg $250,000 after tax. If the current rate of depletion of their savings and investment assets is $9,000 per month, the amount of the taxes would have paid for Ernie's care for 16 months. The decision will hinge on whether or not Ernie will live for 16 months. If he is expected to live longer than 16 months, it would be prudent to transfer the IRA and pay the taxes. The residue of the IRA assets (in excess of the CSRA allowance) would then be sheltered through an annuity to allow Ernie to be Medicaid-eligible.

If you have a large IRA, but your total nest egg is not large enough to fully self-insure (private pay) the long-term care costs, you should have a conversation with your investment advisor or tax advisor as to what it would look like if you rolled your traditional IRA into a Roth IRA, in small annual rollovers over a ten year period, to minimize the income tax rate.

In the above scenario, if after Ernie's retirement, he and Peg had taken steps to roll over approximately $30,000 per year of Ernie's IRA, they would not face such a difficult decision, on top of all the other decisions related to the Accidental Safari. Annual IRA transfers of relatively small amounts would have subjected the rollovers to a much lower tax bracket.

WHAT IF I'M SINGLE?

A single person does not have the same options for asset preservation because they do not have a well spouse to whom they can transfer assets. The maximum amount of cash, savings, and investments allowed for Medicaid qualification for a single person is $2,000. An individual will have to spend down his/her assets to the Medicaid limit of $2,000, at which time Medicaid would begin to pay for care.

In addition to the $2,000 in cash, savings, and investments, a single person may also own the following and still be eligible for Medicaid:

- a home

- a vehicle

- life insurance up to $1,500 in face value

- burial plot and pre-paid funeral

- personal property of any value

A Medicaid recipient can continue to own a residence as long as there is a chance the recipient may return home at a future time. What are the pros and cons of continuing to own and renting out the property versus selling it outright?

If the home is retained and rented out, there is the requirement to, and responsibility for, managing the property. A family member could do this, but the family may already be stretched looking after the Medicaid recipient's needs. Another option would be to use part or all of the rental income to pay a property management company to manage the property and other related costs of property ownership.

There is no income benefit to keeping the property because all net rental income would be added to the Medicaid recipient's income, which is then paid to the nursing home toward the cost of care (less the small personal monthly allowance of $57.00).

Is there a benefit to the Medicaid recipient if he/she still owns the home at the time of death? After the death of the recipient, Medicaid would place a lien on the home, up to the total value of the benefits paid for the recipient's care. The home would have to be sold or mortgaged at that time to pay the lien.

Deciding whether to maintain the residence may depend on a thorough understanding of two key aspects of Medicaid's procedures. First, the Medicaid recipient is ultimately billed less for care than a private pay patient, because Medicaid pays at the Medicaid daily rate not the private daily rate. The difference between these two amounts is about one-third of the daily private pay rate. Second, there is no carrying cost (interest) applied to the benefits that Medicaid pays for care. The eventual payoff of the lien on the residence would not include interest charges. The Medicaid lien would be only for the total amount paid for the recipient's care and would be limited to the amount of the proceeds of the sale of the house, after probate costs and costs of the sale.

Before reaching a conclusion about whether to sell the home, let's consider a real-life situation.

THE SOLO SAFARI

Pat is single. After a sudden medical emergency, Pat was sent to a nursing home. Within a few short months, Pat's savings were gone and Pat was Medicaid-qualified. Pat owns a home worth $200,000.00, and Pat's children suggested the house be rented out to generate net income after taxes and expenses. The rental income would be paid to the homeowner, Pat.

All of Pat's monthly income (less the personal needs allowance of $57.00) would be paid to the nursing home, which was Pat's "participation" in the cost of care.

Should Pat's home be sold? It depends.

If Pat's nursing home stay is anticipated to be for a limited time and Pat might be able to return home with need for ongoing care, and Pat wants to return home, it probably makes sense to keep it.

If Pat's nursing home stay is likely to be lengthy and Pat's cost of care approaches or exceeds the value of the home, it makes sense to sell it. Selling the home during Pat's lifetime could provide additional funds necessary to improve Pat's quality of life. There may be a nursing facility closer to family and loved ones or certain therapies, treatments, and care options that would better address Pat's needs. Funds from the sale of the house could also allow Pat's loved ones to hire a caregiver or care manager so that those closest to Pat are more available to minister hope and love.

If a family member wants to buy the family home, they could purchase it before or after Pat's death, depending on the circumstances. If the home is sold during Pat's lifetime, the proceeds from the sale of the home would send the value of Pat's savings account from under $2,000 to over $200,000. Pat would no longer be eligible for Medicaid and would have to pay privately for care until the balance of the savings account drops below $2,000. There would be no reimbursement to Medicaid for past payments at the time the house was sold. Medicaid would be reimbursed, only after Pat dies, from assets left in the estate, if any.

WHAT IF I'M A VETERAN?

Veteran's benefits are available to individuals who have served in the American Armed Forces. These are basic benefits that all veterans receive if they have been on active duty between 90 days and two years (depending on the benefit) and they received other than a dishonorable discharge.

The Veterans Benefits Administration website at http://www.benefits.va.gov/BENEFITS/factsheets.asp is an excellent place to research the eligibility requirements for the various benefits available to veterans. The home page can direct you to the following resources:

- Fact Sheets:
- General Benefit Information
- Veterans with Service-Connected Disabilities
- Veterans with Limited Income
- Education and Training for Veterans
- Home Loans
- Dependents and Survivors' Benefits
- Insurance
- Fiduciary
- Vocational Rehabilitation and Employment

- Miscellaneous

- Burial and Memorial Benefits

- Military Sexual Trauma

After you have familiarized yourself with the basic benefits and application requirements, you may want to meet with a "veterans benefit specialist," a government employee or volunteer whose job is to help you identify the services you need, explain your eligibility, and instruct you on how to apply for benefits.

You can find a veterans benefit specialist at state or federal veterans' homes or through the Office of Personnel Management (OPM) (https://www.va.gov/osdbu/verification/assistance/counselors.asp). Most of the local branches of the Veterans of Foreign Wars have volunteers who are also trained to provide this type of assistance.

(https://www.legion.org/veteransbenefits)

Benefits are available to address specific issues such as disability compensation, pension, education and training, health care, home loans, insurance, vocational rehabilitation and employment, and burial.

(http://www.benefits.va.gov/PERSONA/veteran-vietnam.asp)

Veterans benefits related to care are divided into two categories: service- related disability and non-service-related disability.

Service-related disabilities are disabilities that are a result of military service. The disability does not need to have been diagnosed during the term of duty.

A person discharged from the service with an identified disability, such as a physical or psychological wound, is assigned a "percentage of disability," which identifies the level of incapacity. The VA offers a package of benefits based on levels of disability. Those benefits could include monthly financial compensation, counseling services, and access to medical and care services.

As stated above, having an identified disability at the time of discharge is not a requirement for eligibility to receive veteran's disability benefits. Many veterans who served in Vietnam were exposed to Agent Orange and other herbicides used to defoliate the jungle. Certain cancers and other health problems are considered presumptive diseases. If a veteran had boots on the ground in Vietnam and displays a listed disease, there is a presumption that the cause of that disease was service related.

(https://www.publichealth.va.gov/exposures/agentorange/conditions/)[12]

Unfortunately, many veterans are not aware of the benefits available to them, or they have chosen not to apply for them. A veteran may be asking himself or herself, "What is my sacrifice compared to those who gave their lives?" This feeling often leads to guilt about seeking and receiving help.

A seventy percent (70%) disability rating is a key threshold as it relates to the eligibility for many veteran's benefits, including payment of long-term care costs. A person who has a 70% disability rating or higher, and needs nursing home care, is eligible for coverage, and care will be provided in a state or federal VA facility. My client, Bill, was one such veteran.

THANK YOU FOR YOUR SERVICE

Bill and Martha came to the appointment, but it was Martha who did most of the talking. I could tell that Bill was having difficulty following the conversation, although he was making a valiant effort to stay engaged.

Bill was forced into retirement, at the age of 59, when he began to show signs of impaired memory. Bill's retirement income would have been higher if he had been able to work up to full retirement age of 66. However, as a machinist, it was extremely important for safety reasons that he be able to maintain sharp focus.

Bill and Martha had a disabled adult son who had always lived with them. Martha had limited work history due to the high care needs of their son. They came to see me because Martha was becoming overwhelmed providing care for both husband and son.

During the meeting, I learned that Bill had spent time in the U.S. Army. At that point, Bill entered the conversation and shared a short, animated story of an event that occurred in Vietnam. It was obvious that he had shared this story many times before, but he had lost pieces of the story along the way and it was impossible for me to make complete sense of it. I could tell that he was very proud of the story and the men in it. I asked a couple of questions for clarification, and Martha filled in pieces of the story to wrap up the loose ends. Bill had a smile on his face, which I was careful to acknowledge.

Bill, it turned out, served two tours in Vietnam as an infantryman. He saw a lot of action and, unfortunately, suffered from Agent Orange exposure. His sacrifice through service led to a significant level of disability.

I explained to Martha that she needed to file a claim for assistance with the Department of Veterans Affairs. She could obtain an application from a local Veterans of Foreign Wars (VFW) chapter or from a VA Benefit Specialist at a local Veterans Hospital or Home. The benefit, once approved, would provide immediate financial assistance and make Bill eligible for care services at home or in a veteran's facility.

Under the disability benefit, Bill would be eligible for full care at the Veterans Home, and his retirement income would not need to go toward his care but could continue to be used to support the family. If you recall, in the case of Ernie and Peg, to qualify Ernie for Medicaid, virtually all of his income had to be paid to the nursing home as his participation in the cost of his care. However, under Bill's disability rating of 70%, Bill would continue to receive his retirement income, and it would be wholly available to meet the needs of Martha and their son. More importantly, in addition to the veteran's benefits available to Bill, Martha and their disabled child were also eligible for benefits that would continue when Bill died. After his death, Martha would receive a survivor benefit from his disability, and her son would receive a disability payment for his lifetime.

There is no way to describe the outcome of our meeting except as life changing. As I explained the benefits available to Bill and Martha, I tried to convey it in such a way that Bill would be able to grasp just how significant his sacrifice on the rice paddies of Vietnam was to his family and to our nation. His service, which included exposure to a poison that would take years off his life, was of inestimable value. Veteran's benefits are a "thank you" from the American people to Bill and others who have served our country through military service. I'll say it again, "Thank you, veterans. Thank you, Bill. We are forever grateful to you, and we promise to take care of you and your loved ones."

Other veteran's benefits are available, but are often overlooked. These include "Homebound" service and "Aid and Attendance." Homebound service pays for assistance to veterans who are confined to their home. Aid and Attendance provides a monthly stipend to veterans to pay for care. Both of these programs are for veterans who have non-service-related disabilities. To qualify, a veteran, or the spouse, has to meet physical, financial, and service eligibility requirements.

The physical requirement to qualify for Homebound services is the inability to leave home without difficulty. To qualify for Aid and Attendance, the applicant must already be living in a care facility or a doctor must provide a written diagnosis that the applicant requires assistance with the activities of daily living.

The financial requirements to receive Homebound services and Aid and Attendance are that the veteran and/or spouse may own a home and a car, and their liquid assets must be between $20,000 and $80,000, depending on the age of the benefit recipient.

The service requirements are that the veteran must have discharge papers (DD-214) that show other than a dishonorable discharge. The veteran must have served at least 90 days of active duty and at least one of those days must have been during a period when the United States was at war. (See Appendix: "Periods of War"). The government web page that describes these programs states that the benefits are paid "in addition to the monthly pension," so Homebound service or Aid and Attendance would be an add-on benefit. An application for these benefits can be found on the website http://www.benefits.va.gov/pension/aid_attendance_housebound.asp or https://www.publichealth.va.gov/about/vemec/projects/pre-paredness-homebound-veterans.asp Because the Homebound service and Aid and Attendance programs provide care and/or financial assistance, they can be a very helpful part of a veteran's care plan. But, because they have asset and income limits for eligibility, they will be applicable in certain, but not all, situations. Coordinating Medicaid and veteran's benefits during the Accidental Safari can be tricky. To save time, I recommend that you have a discussion early on with an expert guide who understands all these programs and who can lead you through the maze of possibilities.

For example, if you are planning to apply for Medicaid, it would be a waste of time, in almost all cases, to apply for Aid and Attendance. The reason for this is that Aid and Attendance pays a monthly stipend to the recipient for monthly care expenses. Once qualified for Medicaid, the person receiving care will pay virtually all of their monthly income to the care facility as their participation in the cost of care. Any additional income that the Medicaid recipient receives from Aid and Attendance would be paid to the facility.

These are very complex areas of the jungle. While they are navigable, you will need to proceed carefully and with recognition of the many interrelated parts that comprise the Life Care Plan.

9

SWISS FAMILY ROBINSON?
NOT EXACTLY

As an experienced guide, I can quickly determine where a client is on the Accidental Safari. Some clients have come to me because they know that preparing a plan is the "smart" thing to do. Others come because they want to take steps to plan for the Safari they see on the horizon. And some have come because they are already on the Safari, but didn't know it until they woke up one morning in the middle of the jungle with survival on the line.

I give credit to people who have the vision to see the reality ahead and the courage to take action. Most people neglect to look ahead, or they are so content with the status quo that they don't want to contemplate a future that might involve change. But change is the only thing that is truly constant, so we'd better expect it and, if possible, embrace it. Change is usually good, but it can be stressful. And it sometimes requires real courage to embrace it. My advice for those facing a significant life change is to see the change for what it is and move forward rather than allow the coming circumstances to control the outcome.

An elder law attorney guides people through the Accidental Safari by helping them understand all the issues related to their medical, housing, financial, and legal needs. I help my clients make decisions from all the available options. For people on the Safari who have done little advance planning, the options may not include their first, second, or even third choice. Once on the Accidental Safari, the choices are limited and the options can be shockingly few.

HOUSING SUSTAINABILITY

Remember, two elements affect the sustainability of the plan: the cost of the plan and the commitment to the plan. A plan *can't* be pursued if there is no way to pay for it, and a plan *won't* be pursued if there is a lack of commitment to follow it. So, even if you have found a way to pay for the Safari, your plan will fail if you lack commitment to the plan. This is often seen in situations where a housing change is needed, but the recommendation is not heeded. Such was the case with Bill and Carol.

BOUGHT THE FARM

Bill and Carol came to my office to prepare an estate plan because they were planners and realists. They were asking the right questions, and our conversation naturally led to a discussion about the issue of Life Care Planning.

Long before retirement, Bill and Carol visited and fell in love with the Pacific Northwest. On an impulse, they purchased five serene acres of land. As the years passed, they visited their "farm" and made plans to build their dream home when they retired.

When they both received retirement offers too good to refuse, enjoyed a strong upturn in the stock market, and sold their home at the top of the local real estate bubble, they knew the time was right to retire. They moved to the farm and lived their dream for almost 25 years.

Bill and Carol loved the ranch style home they built on the farm. They had designed it to allow them to "age in place." There were no staircases. The floor plan was open, with wide doorways. There was only a small lip to step over to access the shower, and they installed grab bars in strategic places for safety.

Bill liked to say that the only way he was moving out of that home was feet first, but they were beginning to see that the "gentleman's farm," as ideal as it was, was becoming more than they could handle. Carol said, "Bill can't repair the fences that need mending and keep up with the blackberries that are taking over the fields." Bill looked at me with a smile that said he would leave unspoken those things that Carol could no longer do.

I made a mental leap, "They are ready to step ahead of the curve and make an intentional decision to leave the farm and prepare for the next stage of their lives!" I was excited for them. I sensed that although this was a bittersweet time for them, they were admitting to me that they needed to seek an alternative living arrangement that would limit or eliminate the outside work for Bill and do the same for Carol and Bill inside the home.

That's when the train came off of the tracks.

Zena. The dog. The third member of the household.

"Zena just loves the yard!"

"Zena has only 4 or 5 more years with us."

They would think about moving, but actually do it after Zena was gone. They couldn't even consider moving into a place with little or no yard now. They didn't know if assisted living places even allowed dogs. Zena was part of the family, and they would not consider a change while Zena was around.

My initial thought was that Zena would have 4 or 5 more years to escape through the broken-down fences, but Bill and Carol probably didn't have 4 or 5 more years to bear the load of caring for such a large property. They were already overwhelmed. They couldn't take care of the things they owned and were growing less able to take care of each other. There would be no better time than the present to work together to extricate themselves from the farm.

What if they should wake up one day to discover that one of them was on an Accidental Safari? What would they do? The well spouse would have no choice but to focus on the all-encompassing needs of the ill spouse. Attention to the farm would end entirely. My thought was, "If they think the wheels are getting ready to fall off the bus now, wait until one of them falls or has some other medical emergency."

Bill and Carol followed through and created an estate plan that covered their future legal needs and positioned themselves for the storm to come. They acknowledged that the best course of action would be to evacuate before the hurricane hit, but they were unwilling to do so. They were going to hunker down and hold on. They were not ignoring the issues. They were acknowledging the elephant in the room. But they made the conscious decision to stay in their home.

It was not the option that I would have chosen for them, but it was not my choice. I did my part to help them understand what the choices were and the likely outcomes they would face. Then, I outfitted them for the path they had chosen.

HOME IS WHERE YOU MAKE IT

Many people resist leaving home. They want to stay in their homes and receive care when they need it. There are several reasons for this, but a common misconception is that this is a less expensive care option. In-home care can actually cost more than nursing care facilities—a lot more. So, when making housing decisions, it is important to remember that sustainability is key. The story below illustrates planning a sequence of options that extended the sustainability of a care plan, which then allowed Millie to remain in her home.

KEEPING THE HOME FIRES BURNING

I was surprised when the elderly gentleman in my office told me that he was there on behalf of his mother, Millie. Millie's deepest desire was to die at home, where she had spent her entire life. Tom was hoping he could he make it happen for her.

Millie was receiving 24-hour care at home. Millie suffered from dementia, and the cost of her home care exceeded $15,000 per month. Her home care costs were not less expensive than care in a facility, but it was in the comfort of her home, which meant everything to her.

Tom was the acting attorney-in-fact under Millie's Power of Attorney. He showed me copies of her current financial statements. Those statements indicated that her monthly income and savings would allow her to stay in her home for approximately three more years before the money would run out. Tom wanted to know what could be done to keep Millie at home if she lived longer than three years.

I inquired about other financial resources that might be available. Millie had no additional resources. Tom, who was beginning to recognize that he had no Life Care Plan of his own, was unable to help Millie financially.

I went over all possible sources of assistance.

Neither Millie, nor her late husband, were veterans, so the Aid and Attendance benefit, which could provide a monthly payment toward non-service related care costs, was unavailable to her.

Tom did not live in Millie's home, so the Medicaid rule that allows the transfer of a residence, without penalty, to a child living in the home with the parent for two years prior to Medicaid eligibility, would also not apply. Although that option would have preserved her home, it would not have provided additional funds to pay for Millie's care.

Tom was not disabled under Social Security rules, so Millie did not qualify to transfer her residence to Tom under the Disability Transfer Exception (which allows assets to be transferred to a disabled child or placed in trust for the benefit of a disabled child) in order to become Medicaid-eligible immediately.

Additionally, Millie's home was fully paid for and, because she was a widow, the title was in her name only. This meant she couldn't take advantage of the Medicaid rule that allows the transfer of a residence to the spouse for immediate Medicaid-eligibility.

Tom was stunned. He asked, "What can we do when the money is gone? It would break my heart for Mom to have to move out of her house."

Sometimes the reality of a situation makes the decision-making process difficult, but relatively straightforward. I said, "If Millie has no resources to pay for her care, the house will have to be sold." I allowed those words to sink in for a minute.

"However," I continued, "What if, before the money runs out, Millie gets a reverse mortgage on the home? That action would generate cash equal to approximately fifty percent of the value of her home." I reached for a calculator. "That cash, plus her regular monthly income, could keep her in her home another 36 months."

(Note: A reverse mortgage is available to homeowners over 62 years of age. It generates income for the homeowner up to a percentage of the equity in the home. A reverse mortgage requires no monthly payments; however, the homeowner continues to own the home, remains responsible for all property taxes, insurance, and maintenance expenses. The home-owner is able to continue to live in the home, without mortgage payments, while paying taxes and insur-ance, until his/her death.)

Tom smiled and asked, "What would we do next, after that?"

I was on a roll. "You would have to sell the home. But what if you sold the house subject to a lease-back, requiring the buyer to lease it back to Millie? She would have to pay rent to the buyer and the reverse mortgage would be paid back from part of the pro-ceeds of the sale. That would leave Millie with about 40 percent of the value of the home, plus her income, which would allow her to stay in the home another 24 to 30 months."

Nodding now, Tom was quick to ask "What would we do next, after that?"

I was thinking that Millie would be about 104 years old at that time. I said, "If Millie is still alive, she would have to go into a care facility and she would qualify for Medicaid to pay for it."

Tom seemed comfortable with that. He left my office with peace of mind and a plan that would likely allow his mother to stay in her home until she died.

Here's a recap of the plan: They would use Millie's money to pay for care until her money was gone. When her money ran out, they would secure a reverse mortgage on the residence. This arrangement, which is sustainable indefinitely or for a very long time in most cases, would not carry Millie for more than approximately 3 years due to her extremely high monthly care costs. At that time, they would sell the property to a buyer willing to lease the home back to Millie. This plan would buy additional time for Millie to remain at home at a critical period of her care. When the lease-back period expired, Millie would have to move out of her home. (Note: Borrowing money for care is never a sound idea, but a reverse mortgage is not borrowing in the traditional sense. Because Millie would be borrowing against the equity in her home, only the house itself would be the collateral to repay the funds after her death.) Millie would move into a care facility with Medicaid as the financial safety net.

The plan worked perfectly and Millie was able to remain at home until her death. The plan also gave peace of mind to Tom, which he was able to pass on to his mother.

INDEPENDENCE: LICENSED TO DRIVE

American culture places a high value on individual freedom and, to many seniors, the exercise of that freedom is best represented by their ability to drive a car. If you want to trigger some strong memories, ask a senior about their first car or their first driving lesson. These memories evoke emotions of freedom and independence because learning to drive was perhaps the first real opportunity they had to spread their wings and fly. It should come as no surprise then that asking a senior to stop driving may evoke a very strong negative response. It may be very difficult to convince them that it is dangerous for them to drive because of the risk of an accident. They'll rationalize that "it won't happen to me." But there will come a time when the wisest course of action is to stop driving.

I mentioned in Chapter 1 that when we were born we needed someone to hold us, feed us, and change our diapers. We also needed someone who could drive us around. If we live long enough, we'll need someone to do all of those things for us again. The graph below confirms this "circle of life" paradigm. The data shows ages below which, and above which, the risk of driving accidents significantly increases. The stories below are examples of senior drivers, from my own experiences.

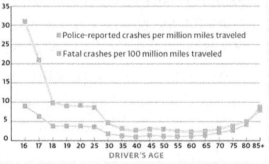

Dangerous curves: Plotting the problem

The youngest and oldest drivers have much higher rates of highway crashes and deaths than any other age group, according to 2008 government mileage data, the latest available. Drivers ages 16 and 17 are involved in more crashes, and fatality rates rise steeply for those older than 65, with drivers older than 80 being most vulnerable.

- Police-reported crashes per million miles traveled
- Fatal crashes per 100 million miles traveled

DRIVER'S AGE

"Reasons Why Teenagers and Older People Are the Riskiest Drivers." Consumer Reports Magazine, October 2012. Based on data from the National Highway Traffic Safety Administration and Insurance Institute for Highway Safety. Retrieved from https://www.consumerreports.org/cro/magazine/2012/10/teenagers-and-older-people-are-the-riskiest-drivers/index.htm

LORD, GIVE ME EYES TO SEE

Ed had driven three hours from his home to pick up his mother and bring her to my office. Occasionally, when a parent and a child reverse roles and the parent becomes the dependent, there can be feelings of resentment and resistance. Ed and his mother, Sharon, realized that the role reversal had occurred but Sharon was accepting, and even grateful, that Ed had stepped up to help her. She was 90 years old and still driving. Ed (and every other driver on the road) was concerned about that.

I had, coincidently, heard a story about Sharon from a third party. She was known to drive herself to church every Sunday morning. She looked forward to meeting with her close circle of friends, just as they had done for many, many, years. One particular Sunday morning, Sharon took the opportunity to offer a prayer request. "Please pray that the Lord would touch my eyes," she said. "The macular degeneration is starting to create waves and spots in my vision. But, thank the Lord, I can still drive!"

Sharon wasn't exactly sure why her prayer request was met with laughter from the group.

I remember a similar story. I used to attend a weekly breakfast meeting. An older gentleman also attended the group. He would always park next to the door of the restaurant in a handicapped parking space. One morning, as I was entering the restaurant, I had a chance to observe him parking his car.

He eased the big Chrysler New Yorker into the parking space until the handicap sign began to bend from the pressure of the car's contact with it. It was a surprisingly big bump. I thought that I would wait and walk in with him.

As he got out of the car, I couldn't help noticing multiple scrapes and dents on the car. He may have anticipated my comment on his parking method, because the first thing he said to me was, "I have a little trouble with depth perception, so it helps me to watch the sign."

What he meant was "I can't see well enough to know when to stop, so I keep going until I hit something." This is not an ideal way to drive a car. I call it driving by Braille.

"Stan," I said, "When you were teaching your kids to drive, did you teach them to keep going until they hit something?" When he didn't laugh with me, I knew I had hit a nerve. (It is also possible that he may not have heard me clearly.) "Stan," I said, "I would be happy to pick you up on Thursday mornings, if you like." He ignored that comment as well.

The stories about seniors driving are funny until you consider that someone you love may one day be on the receiving end of a potentially dangerous driving situation. And seniors who push the envelope on safety are putting themselves and others at serious risk.

Some of the factors to consider when deciding if it's time to hang up the car keys are as follows:

Physical limitations, such as vision and hearing loss, which can lead to accidents. Limitations on the ability to turn one's head can further reduce a driver's ability to hear or see potential dangers on the road or in a parking lot.

Mental limitations, which can affect memory and/or reaction time. These limitations reduce the driver's ability to anticipate danger, avoid distractions, apply focus, and react quickly to changing circumstances.

Medication and alcohol consumption, which can affect the ability to focus and can cause drowsiness.

Reduced muscle and bone strength, which can increase the likelihood of injury or death in what would otherwise be considered a minor accident.

What can you do when a senior resists the call to stop driving? The senior may willingly admit that they are experiencing a minor decline in physical and/or mental ability, but they view driving as a line in the sand that they are unwilling to cross, and you stand between him/her and the car.

You are going to need a plan. I recommend you take the following steps:

Confirm that there is a problem. Don't make driving the "elephant in the room." This is an issue that once recognized, must be addressed. If you have been made aware of the problem ("Your father got another speeding ticket") or you experienced it personally, confirm the reality of the situation. Are there new dents or scratches on the car? Have there been speeding tickets or a sudden increase in insurance premiums? Have there been admissions such as "I don't like to drive at night"?" Document your findings.

Test the waters. Take a ride with the senior. Note the speed. Is the driver going uncomfortably fast or too slow? Take note of everything unusual. If your parent is the senior in question, you should be familiar enough with their driving habits to detect changes. Do they fasten the seat belt? Do they use their phone while driving? If you feel uncomfortable about anything that is happening, make note of it. You are going to have to communicate the issues later, so put it in writing now.

Seek wise counsel. If you believe a problem exists, seek counsel to affirm your assessment of the danger level. Get input on possible ways to approach the subject with the senior. If possible, have conversations with his/her neighbors, doctor, friends, etc. These conversations will either confirm or allay your fears and may lead you to the best individual to have "the conversation" with the senior.

Choose the "bearer of the bad news." If you have not identified an obvious person to initiate the conversation, you must be prepared to do it yourself.

Take action. Have a respectful conversation and present transportation alternatives. To initiate the conversation, you might share a news story about a serious accident involving a senior (easy to find on the internet). Talk about the reasons he/

she should consider giving up driving: finances (the car now needs a big repair or is ready to be replaced), increased insurance costs, physical or mental limitations, and the resultant danger to themselves and others. Let the senior respond, and then present the alternative transportation options once again. These options include:

Friends and family who would commit to being available to provide transportation on a regular basis. (And a second pair of ears at a medical appointment is always a good idea.) If the senior attends a regular meeting, someone from the group may be willing to drive.

Free bus services can be scheduled in advance and on a regular schedule.

Senior service organizations and volunteer groups exist to provide transportation to seniors.

On-call car services such as a taxi, Uber, or Lyft can be cost effective compared to owning, maintaining, and insuring a car driven on a limited basis by a senior driver.

ADDITIONAL BENEFITS OF THIRD-PARTY TRANSPORTATION

There are additional benefits to having transportation provided by a third party. The first benefit is the social contact it provides the senior. Another benefit is that it ensures someone is looking in on the senior on a regular basis, observing his/her appearance and attitude while also keeping an occasional eye on the refrigerator or the prescription bottles.

When a senior stops driving, he or she may experience feelings of loneliness and depression, especially if others do not maintain contact and they begin to lose their connection to relationships and previous sources of entertainment and encouragement.

You may recall the story of my mother's stroke and resulting isolation caused by a wheelchair and two flights of stairs. When I left home for college, my best friends, Richard and Tony, faithfully attended to my mother in my absence. Together, every Sunday for many years, they worked her wheelchair down the stairs of the apartment, pushed it five long blocks to church, and then returned her safely home. I am sure it was the highlight of my mother's week. Even now, as I remember this gift of friendship and their kindness to my mother, I am deeply humbled and forever grateful.

10

ROOM SERVICE PLEASE

You can outsource most jobs around the house. People will mow the grass, clear the gutters, clean the house, do the laundry, and make your meals. They will give you a shower, help you get dressed, and manage your medications and your shopping needs. But a great deal of time, money, and effort is required to coordinate all these services.

Just because it is possible to outsource all this work, doesn't mean that you should. There is a big difference between making choices with intentionality about how your life should be handled and allowing circumstances to determine the choices for you.

THE CHOICE IS YOURS

If your adult children invite you out to dinner at the local "Assisted Living" facility, be warned. The food and the company may be good, but if, after dessert, everyone at the table suddenly leaves to run an errand promising to "come right back," watch out. As the dining room continues to empty, and it grows darker outside, warning lights in your head should be flashing!

If you ask the server, who has graciously offered coffee refills and extra dessert, about your children returning, and she suggests that you might want to lie down for a while in a comfortable room, run for the door!

People usually laugh when I give this warning because the inference is that if you aren't careful, your children may trick you into visiting an assisted living facility and leave you there permanently.

In all seriousness, though, I'm going to suggest that dinner at an assisted living facility may be just what the attorney ordered! If you are considering an assisted living (or similar) facility for a loved one (or even yourself), it is helpful if you are familiar with some of the local facilities and the different levels of care they offer. Of course, the best way to get familiar is to visit them.

CRACKING THE CODE

My first trip to a memory care facility, to visit a client, was memorable (no pun intended) to say the least. The front entry consisted of two doors located a few feet apart. When it was time to leave, I pushed the bar on the first door, which promptly opened, and I walked into the gap between the two doors. I stood there between them, one door in front of me and another door just behind me. To my complete surprise, the door now in front of me didn't open when I pushed the bar. It was locked. I was confused for just a moment, before I remembered that memory facilities are kept locked to prevent residents from wandering away. "Okay," I thought to myself, "That's perfectly reasonable, but how do I get out?"

As I looked around, I noticed a numeric key pad on the wall to the right of the door. I considered the situation for another moment, "Well, that's great; but what's the exit code?"

I stood there for a few additional minutes. I thought about turning around and walking back to the reception desk but, by this time I had a point to prove (the point being that I'd better be able to figure this out on my own). I looked around again but still couldn't find the sign that would offer the key numbers to escape. Then, something small caught my eye. It was a framed poem above the keypad that read

One big old car
Two people in the front seat
Three people in the back
Five people in the car!

"Well, that poem doesn't even rhyme!" I mused. "Now, how do I get out of here?" I could feel perspiration forming on my lip. "Don't panic," I told myself, taking a few deep breaths to regain my composure.

"Oh! Hold on just a minute! The numbers in that silly poem are the secret code to allow me to escape this prison! I'm a regular Sherlock Homes! I guess I don't belong here, yet!"

Good planning always begins by collecting information. If my experience at the memory care center is an example, you'll want to start gathering information early. Reading this book is one way to begin to collect information. Visiting potential care facilities is another way. After all, what better way to gain information about the landscape you'll see on the Safari than to visit it on your own terms? Visiting facilities with the person needing care provides a starting point for the conversation, and it is never too early to begin talking about the Accidental Safari. Information is power. The more you know, the better you can plan. Conversations dissolve fear of the unknown and help build a positive perspective.

Information gathering is a great activity to share with your loved one and can recharge the relationship by providing a new sense of purpose to what may have become routine visits with nothing to talk about. Visiting a local facility together is a good start. A good excuse for the visit may be to take advantage of an interesting activity or entertainment. Of course, if you just want to try out the cafeteria, visiting the facility can begin a conversation and the meal will most likely be free!

Call the facility and ask for a tour and a meal. These facilities spend a lot of money to advertise, so they welcome the opportunity to show you around. Visiting a few different places will expand the conversation exponentially.

A visit with someone who has moved into an independent living or assisted living facility will either bring success or disaster. I suggest that you check with him/her first to be sure that the experience has been positive, for the most part. Unfortunately, horror stories often get more play than the stories of people who have made the transition and are happily enjoying the comforts and services.

Once you have taken a few exploratory trips into the jungle, the conversations will become easier. Invite your loved one to express his/her desires and concerns. Listen to what is being said and take their side as much as possible. Even if the expressed perceptions are inaccurate, continue to have the conversation in order to root out the basis for the fear or misinformation. Be careful not to push too hard toward a desired outcome. If you do, you can expect to feel an amount of push back, if not outright defensiveness and hostility.

If you visit a facility and have a negative experience, let the manager know about it. He/she would want to know. Your honesty will allow them the chance to make it right, and will give you the opportunity to see how they respond to problems or issues that arise. It will also provide a reason to try another facility to compare them. In addition to evaluating the food, consider the amenities, the size of the rooms/apartments, the personal services offered, the costs, and especially the friendliness of the staff.

As you gather information and expand the conversation, your perception of the Accidental Safari will change. Keep in mind that the major reason for doing research is to avoid a situation where a sudden injury or illness forces a hasty decision within a vacuum.

CONSIDERING THE CARE OPTIONS

Many care options exist. These options include the following:

IN-HOME CARE

Personal/health aides can assist with the activities of daily living at home such as bathing, dressing, housekeeping, meals, and shopping.

HOME HEALTH SERVICES

Specific medical services are provided to ill, disabled, or vulnerable individuals in their home. These services include, but are not limited to, nursing care, home health care, physical therapy, occupational therapy, speech therapy, respiratory therapy, nutritional services, and home medical supplies or equipment services.

RESPITE CARE

This option provides a temporary arrangement where care is provided for a specific period of time or for a specific situation. For example, respite would provide care while allowing the primary care giver to take a break, such as for vacation.

ADULT DAY CARE

Adult Day Care programs are available for adults who are able to get out of the home for the day. These programs offer social interaction, meals, and activities such as exercise, games, field trips, art, and music. Transportation is generally provided to and from the day care center. The center may also provide limited medical services such as help taking medications, blood pressure monitoring, and foot care.

INDEPENDENT LIVING

Many communities offer rental apartments designed for adults ages 55 and older. Some independent living facilities offer meals, transportation, housekeeping, and social activities. These communities vary in size and services. They promote a sense of community and connections among the residents.

ASSISTED LIVING

Assisted living facilities offer help with the activities of daily living such as bathing, dressing, and medication administration as well as meals, transportation, housekeeping, and social activities. Some assisted living facilities have an on-site beauty shop, chapel, library, or other amenities. The website http://www.assistedliving.com/laws-by-state/ provides details about assisted living facilities and ombudsmen in each state.

MEMORY CARE

Memory care facilities offer the same services as assisted living facilities to seniors with memory issues. Most memory care facilities are adjacent to an assisted living facility, although the memory care facility is operated independently and will be kept locked down to prevent the residents from leaving the building and wandering into the surrounding neighborhood.

ADULT FAMILY HOME

Adult family homes are frequently overlooked as an option for residential care. They are licensed by the same state agency that oversees other types of facilities. They are limited to a total of two to six residents, and at least one staff person is always on duty, which provides an excellent resident-to-staff ratio. The environment is less institutional than other facilities, and residents may be given an opportunity to assist in many of the daily activities of a normal home such as cooking, setting the table, laundry, or gardening.

Continuing-Care Retirement Community

These communities offer several levels of residential care on one campus: independent living for those who are healthy and active, assisted living for those who need extra help with daily activities, and round-the-clock nursing care for those who are no longer independent. Residents can move among the various levels of care, depending on their needs, yet remain on the same campus. It is important to understand how decisions are made to determine an appropriate level of care, and the resident is allowed significant input in the decision-making process. Continuing-care communities usually require a significant financial down payment or "buy-in." It is important to know how the buy-in funds are held, returned, or forfeited, and it is strongly suggested that prospective residents carefully review or have their representative review all paperwork prior to signing.

Nursing Care

Nursing homes serve three main functions: They provide a place for rehabilitation for people recovering from illness or injury who are either transitioning from the hospital to home or to another facility that offers a lower level of care. These facilities also offer 24-hour nursing care for people who are unable to care for themselves and need long-term care for an extended period. Nursing homes also offer end-of-life care. Services can typically include feeding, dressing, bathing, and toileting, as well as administering medications, wound care, and rehabilitative therapy.

HOSPICE CARE

Hospice focuses on palliative care rather than curative treatment and quality of life rather than quantity of life. A hospice team includes a physician, a nurse, a home health aide, a social worker, a chaplain, and volunteers. Hospice services are available at home or in any of the facilities listed above.

CHOOSING THE RIGHT FACILITY

Selecting a care facility can be challenging because so many options are available. The following questions may facilitate the decision process:

What level of care is needed? Do you or a loved one require assistance with everyday activities, such as getting dressed or walking to the bathroom? Is nursing care needed? Physical or occupational therapy? What does the physician say? Prepare a list of the specialized care services that will be needed.

What type of facility is preferred? Would you or your loved one prefer a small or a large facility? Are there specific living arrangements, such as a single room or double room, that are required? Will meals be taken in a dining room setting or in the resident's room? What amenities are most important? Consider the rules of the facility. Can residents choose when to get up and go to bed? Are visiting hours limited? What social activities are offered? Can residents continue to use their personal physician?

What are the costs? Get all the details on costs, fees, and services. Ask what will be included in the monthly fee and what services are extra. Does the facility accept Medicaid payments? Under what circumstances?

What facilities are available close to home? The importance of location cannot be overstated. Having a loved one in a facility close to home will make a difficult situation tolerable. Continuing to be located close to friends and family can ease the transition to care. If the preferred local facility does not have a vacancy, ask about being added to the waiting list. In any case, do whatever is possible to find a facility close to home. These factors made a tremendous difference when I was faced with the decision about care for my father.

LOCATION, LOCATION, LOCATION

My father was in a nursing home about an hour's drive away from my home. I would go to see him twice a week. Occasionally, I would drive the hour only to find him sleeping. Whether he had been partying very late the night before, was medicated, or just being stubborn, I never knew, but after attempting to wake him and sitting next to his bed for half an hour, I would eventually drive home, without really visiting. It was frustrating.

He had no other advocates in the area. I checked with a local nursing home two minutes from my office to see about moving him there. They had an opening, and we moved him in. It was wonderful. From then on I saw my father almost every day. If he was asleep, I just went back later. No big deal.

I could bring him to my home for a visit and a meal or push his wheelchair to the bakery up the street from the nursing home. I have fond memories of that time, and it all happened because I made the effort to move him to a facility closer to me. We became part of each other's lives again. He was no longer just another obligation that I had to squeeze into my already busy schedule.

What's your first impression? Stop by a facility and walk around on your own. Check it out. Then schedule a formal tour. Get referrals from friends or professionals. Does the facility seem safe? Does the facility pass the smell test? Is the temperature comfortable? What does the staff/resident ratio look like? Are enough caregivers on staff? Are the residents treated respectfully and cheerfully? Is the staff happy and friendly? I recommend that you make an unscheduled follow-up visit to make sure that your first impression was accurate. My first impression of a facility during a recent visit was quite revealing.

A WARM WELCOME

I was visiting a client in a rehabilitation facility early one morning. As I walked to my client's room, I passed six (I was counting) employees. Only one of them said "Good morning" to me. I was looking directly into their faces, giving them a chance to engage me. I was in "their house," so it was their place to extend a greeting and make me feel welcome and at home. This disappointing experience became a red flag.

How does the facility compare with others? The best way to compare facilities is to visit them. Ask everyone you think may have some input what they know about a facility. Contact the local Better Business Bureau or the Division of Aging and Long Term Care to see whether any complaints have been filed, and use websites such as the Nursing Home Compare tool on the Medicare website.

Contact the county "long-term care ombudsman" or the volunteer ombudsman assigned to the facility you are considering. Inquire about specific strengths and weaknesses. A facility ombudsman is a volunteer resident advocate assigned to a particular facility by the county ombudsman. The facility ombudsman gets to know the residents, advocates on their behalf, and investigates resident complaints. The ombudsman is a mandated reporter and, as such, is required to report occurrences of abuse of a resident. To find a local ombudsman, look online for the Division of Aging and Long Term Care, a federal agency with offices in most U.S. counties, or contact your local Agency on Aging.

Get opinions from friends and family who have experience with nursing homes. Ask your doctor for a recommendation if he/she has patients who are resident in a nursing home. Social workers, hospital discharge planners, and local agencies on aging may provide suggestions on facilities that can meet your specific needs and requirements and are located close to you.

Connect with the Admissions Director of the facility early in the process. The Admissions Director can provide you with the necessary information about whether a particular facility can address all the needs of the prospective resident. Ask hard questions related to care and costs. Does the facility have the ability to meet the needs of the resident and the family care manager? What are the costs? If you have Long Term Care Insurance, does it cover the kind of care you want or need? Does the facility accept Medicaid, veteran's benefits, or other third-party payments? Does the facility accept credit card payments? Some credit cards offer cash back, mileage programs, or other perks that could make using the card to make payments attractive; however, never charge payments that you cannot pay in full immediately. Never borrow money to pay the costs of care.

If you are counting on Medicaid to be your safety net, be aware that the system often pushes people to a higher level of care. Medicaid is a federal program administered by the states. States contribute matching funds and are authorized to run the program within the federal guidelines.

In Washington State, where I live and work, if you want to stay at home but you need care, you can apply to the Medicaid program for assistance. The COPES segment of Medicare provides some in-home care, up to a maximum of 5 or 6 hours per day. However, the in-home care program is not designed to provide care at home 24 hours a day, 7 days a week.

I had a client who was a quadriplegic and unable to perform any activities of daily living without total assistance. The maximum number of hours the COPES program could provide was 200 hours per month. Her family wanted her to remain at home, so they filled the gap and provided the necessary 24-hour assistance.

Individuals who do not have a family to act as a safety net would not be able to stay at home. They would have to move into a care facility. If the level of care required is such that the individual could live in a memory care or assisted living facility, it would be less expensive for Medicaid, which would pay the cost of care.

However, most of the assisted living and memory care facilities are privately owned, for-profit businesses. They either do not take Medicaid or they require a two-year (or longer) stay at the private pay rate before a resident can switch to Medicaid (COPES) to pay for care. During the initial two years, if the resident does not have sufficient monthly income to meet the private pay rate, the resident must pay out of savings. If they don't have sufficient savings to pay for two years and the family is unable to help, this part of the program will not be able to meet their needs.

Many of those whose initial preference was for in-home care but couldn't manage it, and whose second choice is assisted living or memory care but can't afford the two-year private pay requirement, are subsequently pushed into an even higher level of care at a nursing facility.

Most nursing facilities will accept Medicaid as payment for care. The system, thankfully, provides a care safety net at the highest level of care and the most expensive cost of care.

11

LIONS AND TIGERS, OH MY

A major difference between lions and tigers in the wild is that lions live in groups, called prides, while tigers live alone. It's the same with people. Some are highly connected; they have friends and acquaintances and are part of a church, service organization, or other association that has enabled them to make lots of connections.

Others are more like tigers. They are introverts or loners, and they enjoy living solitary lives.

There will come a time in life, however, when we need to belong to a pride consisting of a few good friends. We need people who will step up, step in, and help us. These people may become our vital support network as we age.

DEPENDENT ON THE PRIDE

The reality is that many seniors do, in fact, live alone and are alone. Let's compare some relevant statistics from the 1990's with current numbers to confirm the trends. A consequence of women living longer, on average, than men is the relative scarcity of single senior men. The fact is that women are much more likely than men to live alone. So much more likely, in fact, that 8 out of 10 non-institutionalized seniors who lived alone in 1993 were women. Among both sexes, the likelihood of living alone increases with age. The 1993 data show that the likelihood of women living alone rose from thirty-two percent for 65–74 year old women to fifty-seven percent for women over the age of 85. The corresponding rates for men in these age categories were thirteen percent and twenty-nine percent.

(https://www.census.gov/population/socdemo/statbriefs/ agebrief.html)[13]

Many seniors also face dependency. Although the elderly are living longer, is the overall health of the elderly also improving? Poor health among the elderly is not as prevalent as many assume. In 1992, about three out of every four non-institutionalized adults between the ages of 65 and 74 considered their health to be good. Two out of three over the age of 75 felt similarly.

As the Baby Boomers grow older, however, more and more will face chronic illness and limiting conditions. These conditions will result in people becoming dependent upon others for help in performing the activities of daily living. With age comes an increased risk of dependency. For example, while a mere one percent of seniors between the ages of 65 and 74 lived in a nursing home in 1990, nearly one out of four adults 85 years and older did. And among those who were *not* institutionalized in 1990 and 1991, nine percent were between 65 and 69 years old, while fifty percent of those over 85 needed assistance performing everyday activities such as bathing, mobility, and meal preparation.[14]

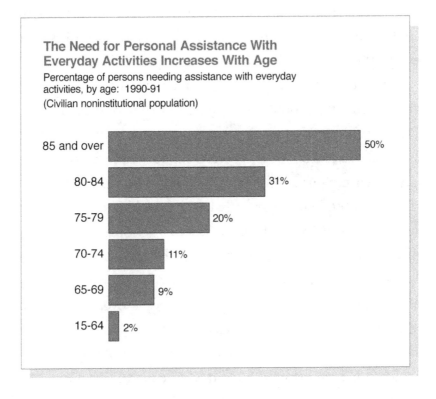

The Need for Personal Assistance With Everyday Activities Increases With Age
Percentage of persons needing assistance with everyday activities, by age: 1990-91
(Civilian noninstitutional population)

U.S. Census Bureau Statistical Brief, May 1995. Economic and Statistics Administration, U.S. Department of Commerce.

It is undeniable that more people are living long enough to eventually experience chronic illness, disability, and dependency. As the population ages, we can expect an increase in the number of individuals between 50 and 60 years of age who will be faced with the responsibility of managing care for their parents. The parent-support ratio gives us an approximate idea of what is to come. This ratio compares the number of persons over age 85 per 100 persons between the ages of 50 to 64 in the general population. Between 1950 and 1993, the ratio tripled from 3 to 10 people over 85 for every 100 persons ages 50 to 64. Over the following six decades, the ratio is expected to triple again, to a whopping 29 people over the age of 85 for every 100 people who are between the ages of 50 and 64.[15]

In 2015, The United Nations Department of Economic and Social Affairs published a Revision of World Population Prospects Report. The report was consistent with the 1993 study above. In 2050, the parent-support ratio in the more developed nations is projected to reach 28%, up from 9% in the year 2000. France currently has the world's highest parent-support ratio at 13% (which equates to 13 people over 85 years of age for every 100 people between the ages of 50 and 64.) By 2050, Japan is projected to have, by far, the world's highest parent-support ratio at 56% (56 people over 85 years of age for every 100 people between the ages 50 and 64). In that same year, the number of people over 85 years of age for every hundred people between 50 and 64 is expected to surpass 30 in another 15 countries, predominantly European.

This phenomenon is developing rapidly in countries that have had the lowest birth rates during the past 60 years. The result is that these countries will not have a younger generation large enough to assist the elderly populace.

As people age, the need for assistance increases. The large number of Baby Boomers, who are living longer, coupled with a shrinking birth rate, will result in more people needing care and fewer people to care for them. The fortunate will have a support network or family who will step in and fill the need.

Ideally, each of us should take responsibility to reach out to those who are aging around us as well as developing a circle of friends, neighbors, and family who will assist with our own future needs.

Sometimes life happens, and we find ourselves alone. What then? Are state or federal programs available to help? Yes, assisted living facilities, nursing homes, and Medicaid were primarily developed as answers to this problem. But what can be done about the elderly who want to live independently at home, but whose circle of support has dwindled or disappeared? Who will be there for them?

A circle of support will need to arise, ideally from the community in which the senior lives. Some communities are already creating this type of support.

There is no single answer to this problem. Religious groups, non-profits, veterans groups, and community service organizations must respond by providing assistance. We need new and innovative ways to bring people together to create community and offer services.

I see many seniors who are facing the challenges discussed here. Unless their circumstances change radically, they are likely to become vulnerable adults, "elder orphans" who are easy prey for perpetrators of abuse.

ALONE AND VULNERABLE

As a person's circle of support gets smaller and eventually disappears, people naturally look for a familiar, or at least a friendly, face to provide help. This situation opens the door to potential elder abuse. Seniors who are isolated, needy, and without a true advocate, are vulnerable.

Imagine that you are traveling alone on the Safari and do not know where to turn. If your jeep stalls, you'll be grateful to anyone who comes along and offers help. If he smiles, invites you into his jeep, and offers to take you to his house for dinner, you may not realize that in this particular country that means he is planning to eat you for dinner. An unsuspecting senior can be easy prey for a dangerous predator.

Elder abuse of any kind deserves our attention. Statistics say that more than 2 million elderly people suffer some form of abuse every year. Those are just the reported cases. The median age of the victim is 78, and the rates of abuse are 57% from neglect, 16% from physical abuse, 12% from financial abuse, and 7% from emotional abuse. (http://www.statisticbrain.com/elderly-abuse-statistics/)[16]

You may be asking yourself—who are the perpetrators of this abuse? Let's look at the areas of abuse listed above.

Neglect. Neglect represents 57% of all abuse cases. It is the biggest challenge because of the sheer numbers. Neglect is defined as the "absence of care." Neglect can be self-inflicted or the result of caregiver abuse and there are a few common warning signs.

Surprisingly, more than half of the reported cases of abuse from neglect are attributed to self-neglect. There is no actual perpetrator: the aging person is simply losing the ability to recognize or respond to his/her own physical, medical, or personal needs.

By far, most caregiver neglect/abuse is at the hands of a family member. The family caregiver is often untrained, overworked, and exhausted. Often, he or she is not accountable to anyone, and difficult situations can deteriorate quickly. Caregivers from legitimate agencies are usually monitored and rotated in a way that prevents caregiver abuse.

Familiarizing yourself with a few common warning signs of self-neglect and/or caregiver neglect/abuse can often prevent further abuse from taking place. Older people do not always report abuse because they may be embarrassed, afraid, or unable to do so. Some may not even realize that they are being neglected. Here are some signs of neglect:

- Absence of necessities including food, water, and heat

- Untreated or unexplained worsening of medical or mental conditions

- Inadequate living environment evidenced by lack of utilities, sufficient space, and ventilation

- Animal or insect infestations

- Medication mismanagement, including empty or unmarked bottles or outdated prescriptions (Note: Persons aged 65 years and older comprise 13% of the population, yet account for more than 33% of total outpatient spending on prescription medications in the United States.) (https://www.drugabuse.gov/publications/research-reports/prescription-drugs/trends-in-prescription-drug-abuse/older-adults)[17]

- Unsafe living conditions due to disrepair, faulty wiring, inadequate sanitation, substandard cleanliness, or architectural barriers

- Unexplained injuries or implausible explanations for injuries

- Dehydration or malnutrition evidenced by weight loss, extreme thirst, low urinary output, dry skin and mouth, sore mouth, apathy, lack of energy, or mental confusion

- Poor personal hygiene

- Untreated bedsores

- Unclothed or improperly clothed for weather

- Extreme withdrawal or agitation

- Absence of needed dentures, eyeglasses, hearing aids, walkers, wheelchairs, braces, or commodes

- Confusion

- Depression

- Nightmares or insomnia

- Aggressive or self-destructive behavior

- Emotional distress

- Ambivalent feelings toward caregivers or family members

(https://www.psychologytoday.com/conditions/elder-or-dependent-adult-neglect) [18]

Physical Abuse. Physical abuse is the next most common type of elder abuse, representing 16% of abuse cases. The perpetrator of physical abuse is generally someone close to the victim or living with the victim, which means the abuser is most likely a close friend or relative, adult child, niece, or nephew. This caregiver is often single, unemployed, and may have substance abuse problems.

Some of the indicators of physical abuse are bruises, bandages, cigarette burns, and even extra articles of clothing to cover areas of the body. The victim might have a limp or a sling or favor a certain area of the body. Multicolored bruises can indicate that they were received over time. Look for bleeding or dried blood around the ears or other body openings. Volunteer to do the laundry, and check for dried blood on clothing. Pattern bruising may also exist around the wrist or upper arm to indicate the use of restraint, tight holding, or grabbing. Falls are common among the elderly, so realize that all bruising is not physical abuse, but look for a pattern of physical injury accompanied by behavioral signs.

The behavioral signs accompanying physical abuse could include the inability of the victim to explain the injury or conflicting stories among the household as to how the injury or injuries occurred. Inquire about the medical follow-up to "injuries" and the length of time between the injury and seeking medical help. A delay in seeking medical help for an obvious injury should cause concern. If a number of incidents occurred, has the victim been brought to different medical facilities to limit the ability of the medical professionals to see a pattern of injury?

Whenever possible in a care situation, a team of caregivers is best. A team provides the respite and accountability that protects both the caregivers and the care receiver.

Financial abuse accounts for approximately 12% of cases of senior abuse but most people would guess that percentage to be higher. It is likely that financial abuse is under reported.

A family member is the perpetrator of financial abuse in 90% of reported cases and, in two-thirds of those cases, the perpetrators are adult children or spouses of the victim.

The potential for financial abuse by a family member suggests that certain protocols and safeguards need to be put in place when a family member becomes the primarily caregiver for a parent. Some of the questions to ask are

1. Should the child receive payment for providing care?

2. How much compensation is reasonable?

3. Is the decision different if the child must leave a good job to provide care?

4. Is the decision different if the child has experienced financial challenges?

5. If it would cost $7,000 per month to hire an agency to provide a full-time caregiver, should the child be paid the same amount for providing full-time care?

6. What oversight should be set in place to protect the caregiver's and the parent's financial assets?

Answering these and other questions will hopefully lead to consensus among family members. In addition to the appointment of a caregiver, an independent party should also be named to provide support and accountability for both the caregiver and the parent. This accountability could be as simple as sharing the monthly bank statements with the independent party.

Given the explosion in the number of elder orphans today, if these issues cannot be adequately addressed by the senior's family, they will need to be addressed by friends or the community in which the senior lives. Each of us should intentionally help our neighbors as best we can.

Unfortunately, there is a growing cadre of scammers and identity thieves around the world, and the senior population is a primary target. Modern methods of communication allow these undesirables access right under our noses, and vulnerable seniors are particularly susceptible to victimization.

The following two examples illustrate common financial abuse scenarios:

THE WINNING TICKET

Maggie was a widow who had been well provided for by her deceased husband. She got along well with her children and grandchildren and was proud to be a great-grandmother.

When she received a phone call from someone posing as a representative of the Publishers Clearing House Giveaway, the hook was set. Maggie was instructed to provide some personal information and send $2,500 to qualify for the finals. She complied quickly—too quickly.

The scammers called back to inform her that she was the big winner! They told her they would send a camera crew to film her receiving the multi-million dollar check. They created an elaborate plan. She would trick her family into coming to her house. When the camera crew knocked on the door, the host would surprise her with the check and everyone would be shocked and overjoyed! For the plan to work, she had to promise not to tell anyone about the surprise. And, by the way, she would need to send $65,000 to pay the preliminary taxes and transportation costs for the camera crew and equipment.

Maggie contacted her investment advisor immediately to give instructions for the sale of securities so the cash would be available in her money market account. He was suspicious at this uncharacteristic behavior and pressed her for the reason. She said she had a special surprise for her children. He was not convinced and made a note in her file to cover his actions.

The money was sent. Immediately, Maggie had second thoughts, but she didn't discuss them with anyone. She wanted to believe it was all true.

As the days passed, she grew more and more embarrassed and depressed. Her daughter asked what was wrong, and she explained it all. The police were called, but not in time to recover any of the money. I wish Maggie's experience was an isolated story, but it isn't.

OPPORTUNITY KNOCKS

Joseph was a healthy 79-year-old retired military officer. He was a widower continuing to live in the family's waterfront home. He enjoyed golf regularly and even managed one of the annual golf tournaments at the club. He was not feeble or of diminished capacity.

The con artist made contact with Joseph through an email phishing expedition. These scams frequently originate in a foreign country and offer a grand payout—millions of dollars—in exchange for assistance in getting money out of the foreign country.

Joseph bit the hook. He was convinced that the Nigerian contact was telling the truth. Millions of dollars needed to be transferred out of Nigeria, and Joseph could get a share if he would help. All he had to do was to work through the system, fill out the paperwork, and pay the fees. Then the big money would be his— a family legacy, he thought.

He was close to his children. They lived in the area and were very involved in each other's lives. His daughter, Kari, had helped him set up his computer. Fortunately, she had remote access to his computer, which allowed her to help him with online financial payments and the like.

Kari had not looked at her father's bank statement in a while, but was surprised to see a dramatic drop in the balance. As she looked back, she saw that two large wire transfers had been made. The first one was in the amount of ten thousand dollars and took place five weeks ago. The second one was for fifty thousand dollars and occurred two weeks ago. She immediately called her brother, Jim. He had no inkling, but agreed to visit his father the next day.

Jim was unsure how to approach the subject because he was uncertain how his father would react. He finally came out and asked his dad if he had made some large purchases recently. His father was excited to tell his son how fortunate they were to be able to cash in on this great opportunity.

Joseph said that a bank officer in Nigeria needed an American citizen to help transfer an account that had been established by a foreigner. The banker thought it may have been drug money, but the depositor had been killed in a plane crash four years ago, and no one had claimed the money. Because there has been no activity in the account, it was going to escheat to the country within the next year if it remained unclaimed. He said that he was the stateside contact to set up the transfer of funds.

Joseph said that he had to send money to pay the taxes due on the account's earnings, as well as other costs and fees. He told Jim not to worry, that all his funds would be reimbursed when he received his share of the account. His share would be 14 million dollars.

The more Jim questioned his father, the more Joseph became defensive. The conversation quickly deteriorated into an argument. Joseph truly believed he had the opportunity of a lifetime, and Jim was raining on his parade.

Jim and Kari didn't know what to do. Joseph had become closed mouth and would speak to no one. Jim and Kari were hoping the issue would just go away.

Jim came to see me after Joseph made another $20,000 transfer. He was at a loss as to what to do. I told Jim that the only way he could block his father's access to his funds was by court order and that someone would still need access to the funds to pay Joseph's living expenses. A guardianship action was the only option.

The guardianship petition was filed with the court, and an immediate order was granted that blocked Joseph's accounts. The order also appointed a Guardian ad Litem (GAL) who would investigate Joseph's situation and make a recommendation to the court about his ability to manage his financial affairs. (A Guardian Ad Litem acts in a temporary capacity until the particular court case is closed.) A hearing was scheduled in ten days to allow Joseph the opportunity to explain to the court why his funds should be unblocked.

The Guardian Ad Litem got right to work and visited Joseph. He told Joseph what the Court's order stated and asked Joseph for his side of the story. Joseph explained all that had happened.

The GAL explained the scam to Joseph and showed him the U. S. State Department's website specifically addressing "the Nigerian scam." The website names individuals who have gone to Nigeria to pick up their share of the money and are now missing. Joseph told the GAL that he was embarrassed that he could have been so naive. He deeply regretted the horrible and expensive mistake he had made.

Convinced that Joseph had seen the error of his ways, the GAL called me to say that he would be recommending that the petition for guardianship be dismissed by the court and Joseph's accounts unblocked. He said that Joseph was an intelligent man who did not require a guardian. He had seen the light and humbly acknowledged his foolishness.

I called my client, Jim, to give him the good news, which he quickly shared with his sister. Kari called me shortly after that call. She had accessed Joseph's email account and was shocked to discover that shortly after the GAL had met with Joseph, Joseph had emailed his Nigerian connection. He told the Nigerian that he had just convinced the court representative that all was well, and he expected that his accounts would be unblocked within the next week. He confirmed that he would transfer the additional funds as soon as possible.

Kari sent a copy of the email to me, which I then forwarded to the GAL. He quickly realized that he had been fooled and that Joseph needed immediate protection. The GAL's report to the court recommended the appointment of a professional guardian who would, thereafter, manage Joseph's finances and make financial decisions on his behalf.

At the hearing, the judge ordered a limited guardianship. Joseph would no longer have direct access to his assets. Joseph was unwavering. He swore at his son at the court hearing and verbally berated and disowned him for ruining the family legacy.

When the guardian took over Joseph's finances, he discovered that Joseph had been preparing to refinance his home in order to send a large payment to Nigeria. The guardian now controlled all of Joseph's funds. The guardian paid Joseph's living expenses and gave him a few hundred dollars a month for spending money. Joseph continued to send two hundred dollars every month to Nigeria.

I discussed this case with a geriatric counselor. She explained that a medical syndrome exists that can create a blind spot to reality. She told me about a client who believed she was dating Kevin Costner. The client would go into great detail about their conversations and activities. She was intelligent and normal in every other area of her life, but she had never actually met Kevin Costner. She refused to see reality in that one area of her life.

You may be asking yourself how anyone could fall for a con like this. The answer is simply that they wanted to. The internet has spawned many criminal schemes. A con artist can "phish" in a pond containing millions of potential victims, at no cost. The "success rate" of these scams is difficult to gauge. One scam artist estimated that he received approximately seven replies per 500 emails he sent. He said that his success rate was 70% of those who replied.(https://en.wikipedia.org/wiki/Advance-fee_scam)[19]

Emotional Abuse. Emotional abuse accounts for approximately 7% of cases of senior abuse. As in other forms of abuse, emotional abuse is usually perpetrated by those closest to the victim. It is often the sole caregiver who intentionally terrorizes the victim through threats, humiliation, and intimidation. It is common for the victim to be isolated from all outside relationships to magnify the control of the abuser over the victim. The abuser will strongly resist efforts to provide respite for themselves or a temporary change or respite to the senior.

Warning Signs. The harm is internal, so the signs are subtle. Look for changes in communication style or a shutdown of communication. Is there resistance to touch or a lack of interest in things that once were compelling to the senior? Depression, confusion, and agitation are all emotions that are common with this kind of abuse.

CARING FOR THE 500-POUND GORILLA

Where does a five-hundred-pound gorilla sit? Answer: Wherever he wants! It is all too easy to refuse help to someone who says they want no help or doesn't receive help graciously. Seniors who are experiencing growing dementia are not themselves. They are frequently out of control, and their inability to recognize and adapt to everyday situations can place them in dire circumstances.

Unfortunately, many seniors fit this description and live as "elder orphans." Like tigers in the wild, they prefer to be alone and are fiercely independent. As a result, they are easily neglected, frequently abandoned, and extremely vulnerable to predators who will happily endure the tiger's claws to gain access to his treasure.

If you are struggling to help a tiger, or if you are a tiger, I advise you to seek out responsible people in the area where you need help. You might ask your neighbor, doctor, pastor, lawyer, or investment advisor for a referral. If the cost of the much-needed service is the problem, consult the local office of the Area Agency on Aging. They can and will connect you to many available services. They can also direct you to a social worker who is able to make arrangements for services. You may also need to contact Adult Protective Services to ensure the safety of a vulnerable senior.

I hear many stories from adult children whose parents need extra help. In many cases, the parent will refuse to admit that they need help and would never agree to pay for the help even when they could easily afford it. Frequently, if an adult child introduces a caregiver into the parent's home to provide assistance, the parent will absolutely refuse their help—even when the child is willing to pay all the expenses.

This situation can place the adult child in a difficult situation with siblings and authorities. The child living nearest to mom and dad often becomes the default overseer of the parents.

If a parent is strong willed and independent, but is failing in mental or physical ability, the situation is especially challenging. Parents may try to hang onto their independence as their physical and mental abilities decline. Although they may be failing to the point that you are concerned for their health and safety, you may not be able get them to accept your help. You might even find yourself unwelcome in their home. *Consider the hypothetical scenario below, for example.*

SUSPECTED OF ABUSE

Imagine that your mother's friend, Claire, who has not seen your mother in several months, stops in to visit and finds her looking gaunt. She hasn't bathed since you were there five days ago, when she kicked you out for suggesting that she hire a caregiver to help her with bathing. Her clothes are soiled, her bed linens are soiled, and old food and dirty dishes remain on the table. She may even have a few bruises on her arms and face from a recent fall.

Your mother, who is having a particularly bad day, cannot remember your last visit. She states that she hasn't seen you in weeks and that all you want to do is spend her money. She may have mixed up her medications, or not taken them. She might be dehydrated or have a urinary tract infection (UTI). These conditions may suggest advanced dementia, even when that is not the problem.

Claire doesn't want to leave your mother alone, but your mother won't allow Claire to call you. Running out of options, Claire dials 9-1-1. The police and ambulance arrive and take your mom to the hospital. Adult Protective Services (APS) is called.

APS contacts you saying that your mother is in the hospital and will be moved to a nursing home after she has been "evaluated and her condition is stable." With "your mother's permission," they have already gone through her home, and pictures were taken showing the soiled bed, dirty dishes, unwashed laundry, and messy bathroom. They may have taken financial records to determine the level of financial abuse that may or may not have taken place.

On the phone, you try to explain that you were just there last Sunday. (It is now Friday.) You explain that she was fine, you see her every weekend, you set up her pill dispenser, get her groceries, and leave her with prepared meals. She wants no outside help. You are named as the attorney-in-fact (agent) in her Powers of Attorney for Health Care and Asset Management.

APS still needs to interview you. They tell you where she is and advise that you can visit her, but that she will stay there, "where it's safe," while they investigate.

When you see your mother, she is still in a mental fog. Her condition will hopefully improve as her medications are adjusted, or the antibiotics help with the urinary tract infection, or she gets rehydrated. Unfortunately, given her present condition, there is no guarantee that she will be glad to see you when you arrive. She may blame you for all the drama and expense. She may launch into a tirade about all the things she has suffered at your hands. And all this information will filter down to APS.

How did this happen? You were totally blindsided. Mom has entered the Accidental Safari at full speed and, like it or not, you are along for the journey. How did you get in this situation? What could you have done to avoid it?

EXPANDING THE CIRCLE OF PROTECTION

In dealing with seniors, never make it a habit to act alone. As often as is practical, have someone assist you. Keep a log of your activities and, whenever possible, share your log with someone who is connected to the senior. If you are assisting a parent, send emails on a regular basis to your siblings, aunts and uncles, cousins, or friends about what actions you are taking to help your parent. Have some independent person, who understands that you are being accountable to them, be a regular contact.

As the story above illustrates, circumstances can spiral out of control rapidly. If you are in a similar situation, ask a geriatric care manager to do an assessment of the senior and his/her living conditions. This assessment will provide an independent evaluation of the situation and the role you are playing in it. If practical, once a baseline is established, have the geriatric care manager perform monthly or quarterly visits to update the status. It will be worth the expense to have a regular, independent, professional assessment. It is all too tempting and easy to ignore or deny the decline in someone you see frequently. At the same time, it is not uncommon for family members visiting a parent's home for the holidays to be shocked at the deteriorating conditions, while local family members see nothing alarming.

If money is involved, always keep someone else in the loop. You should be named as the attorney-in-fact on a Power of Attorney and/or legally appointed by the senior as a named co-signer on the senior's financial accounts if you are managing their money. It is wise to ask the senior to name the individuals who should be included in the information "loop." If you are not authorized, in writing, do not act independently to spend or take money.

If the senior is uncooperative with your request to add an accountability partner, you must insist on having conversations with the investment advisor, the bank manager, or a sibling. It is best to have a credible, independent person in the medical and/or financial area who will, if the need arises, confirm that you have acted responsibly and sought professional help in your effort to manage the care and finances of the senior.

Expanding your circle increases the number of individuals keeping watch over the senior and expands the possibility of additional assistance for you. Admittedly, the larger the circle, the greater is the communication requirement and the potential for disagreement among the parties. A Power of Attorney will be useful to draw clear lines of authority within the team.

As I stated previously, there are two kinds of seniors: the lions and the tigers. The lions have social connections. They attract people who can assist them when the going gets tough. The lion may have paid it forward; may have money; or may simply be an extroverted person. People are drawn to lions. Although lions may be potentially vulnerable, their support circle is usually robust enough to make it difficult for someone to secretly take advantage of them.

Tigers, on the other hand, are seniors who need help, but don't want it. Some need help and would welcome the help, but don't know how to ask for it. And some need help, but don't know that they need help. They are generally introverts and loners. Unfortunately, caring people are not instinctively

drawn to tigers, who may be hyper-independent. They may cling tightly to their sense of privacy and control. In reality, tigers are often the most vulnerable among us, because they fly under the radar. They may not have always been loners. Their connections may have died or moved away. They cannot name a single advocate to act as attorney-in-fact under a Power of Attorney. They are too tired, scared, or introverted to accept help, even from family members.

"Where there's hope, there's life. It fills us with fresh courage and makes us strong again. We'll need to be brave to endure the many fears and hardships and the suffering yet to come."

— Anne Frank, The Diary of a Young Girl

12

THE SAFARI IS ONLY PART
OF THE JOURNEY

The Accidental Safari is only a small part of life's journey, but it gives us an opportunity to finish well.

THE HOPE WITHIN AND WITHOUT

Life doesn't always work out the way we planned. This outcome could be the consequence of wrong actions and poor choices. But sometimes there is no one, and nothing, to blame. Life can just seem unfair and out of our control. Although Long Term Care Insurance, Medicaid, and Veteran's benefits, and other programs, both public and private, can provide aid on the Accidental Safari, no program or benefit, can give us back the control we once thought we had over our lives.

It's our nature to feel that we have things well in hand—until something completely unexpected happens. Some of us will throw up our hands and surrender to the mindless, purposeless forces we believe have taken over our lives. Some will shake their fists at heaven and ask, "How could God have let this happen?" Others will move beyond the anger and disap-pointment and look for hope and meaning outside of them-selves and place their hope in something or someone who has greater power than we do.

The Accidental Safari's gut-wrenching drama works the rich soil of our soul. Hope isn't necessary when you are getting what you want out of life. But hope is a valuable companion in the valleys marked by the shadows of death, the place where what you have is being slowly taken from you.

As you begin to plan for the Accidental Safari that may come, it is important to consider where you have placed your hope. I work with people every day who are in various stages of the Safari. They are searching for hope on the journey.

The Serenity Prayer was written by American theologian Reinhold Niebuhr. It expresses that call for hope and content-ment from many who are on the journey or assisting others along the way:

SERENITY PRAYER

God grant me the serenity
to accept the things I cannot change;
courage to change the things I can;
and wisdom to know the difference.
Living one day at a time;
Enjoying one moment at a time;
Accepting hardships as the pathway to peace;
Taking, as He did, this sinful world
as it is, not as I would have it;
Trusting that He will make all things right

if I surrender to His Will;
That I may be reasonably happy in this life
and supremely happy with Him
Forever in the next.
Amen.

A LIVING HOPE

As the Serenity Prayer so beautifully expresses, hope is an essential tool on the Accidental Safari. Our lives are a richly-woven tapestry of personal connections, events, opportunities, failures and successes. Sadly, on the Safari we often see only the tangled, broken, and knotted threads in the back of the tapestry and fail to catch a glimpse of the beautiful picture being created on the other side. During the Safari that swept my family away when I was a young boy, I held tightly to the faith that God was in control and was weaving a beautiful tapestry from the loose threads of my life. In difficult times, we can hold tightly to God and experience the living hope that comes from placing our trust in Him alone.

> "Be joyful in hope, patient in affliction, faithful in prayer."
> — Romans 12:12

Dr. Henry Van Dyke was a minister and short story writer in the early years of the twentieth century. After hearing the details of the sinking of the Titanic, he wrote a letter of consolation to the survivors, in which he tried to answer the question, "Why do some live on while others die?" He wrote, "It is the ideal of self-sacrifice. It is the rule that 'the strong ought to bear the infirmities of those that are weak....' Only through the belief that the strong are bound to protect and save the weak because *God wills* it so, can we hope to keep self-sacrifice, and love, and heroism, and all the things that make us glad to live and not afraid to die."

On an Accidental Safari, the essential "thing" that makes us glad to live and not afraid to die is the hope that "God wills"—that the loving God of the universe is ultimately in control, and He does all things well according to His will. This is contrary to the common belief in our culture that the strong should take advantage of the weak because "survival of the fittest" demands that the weak, the old, and the disabled should be minimized or eliminated. This view devalues life and extinguishes hope.

Travel any distance with someone on an Accidental Safari, and it is obvious that the qualities needed to survive and thrive are self-sacrifice, heroism, and strength. These qualities make us glad to live and not afraid to die and prove that life itself is precious. The story of Wally and Kathleen beautifully illustrates how a shared Safari can be a blessing both to those on the journey and to those who witness that journey:

A PORTRAIT OF HOPE

I met Wally and Kathleen Nelson several years ago. They had donated a beautiful painting, which Wally himself had painted, to a charity auction that I attended.

Wally was a former Marine, who stood tall in the crowded room. He was a quiet man with a brilliant smile. Wally wouldn't have seemed nearly so quiet had he not been standing next to Kathleen. She stood almost as tall as Wally and had a bright countenance that lit the room. She was proud of Wally and his painting as I expressed my appreciation of the work. At the end of the evening, I received an invitation from Kathleen to visit their home to see some of Wally's other paintings.

I'm not sure what I expected as we headed to their home, but the experience was a surprising look into their lives. We pulled up in front of a modest manufactured home in a nicely groomed mobile home park. Kathleen had prepared afternoon tea.

Kathleen had arranged a dozen of Wally's paintings and, as she showed them, she explained how each one had come to be. The paintings represented a mosaic of their years together—the things they had done and the places they had traveled, as seen through Wally's eyes and artful hands.

Wally sat quietly in the doorway of the room. As Kathleen told the story of each painting, Wally would nod his head now and then, as if playing a part he had rehearsed many times. She would pause and smile at him, and he would occasionally finish her sentences with the perfect punch line. I was fascinated by the stories and how Kathleen's description of each picture that Wally had painted was allowing me to become a part of their experiences. It occurred to me that we had actually been invited into their hearts, which were many times larger than the room we occupied.

Wally was the artist, but Kathleen was the saleslady. He was carefree; she was the bookkeeper. Over the years she had carefully saved so they could enjoy these experiences. They were soulmates and had enjoyed every moment of their life together.

Wally and Kathleen recently celebrated their 62nd wedding anniversary. Kathleen told me that it was beautiful day. The warm sun was shining on the table for two under a spreading magnolia tree at the local Italian restaurant. "It was perfect!" she said. After lunch, Kathleen wheeled Wally the few blocks back to the nursing home where he now lives with Alzheimer's disease.

Kathleen and Wally have traveled a long and meaningful journey together. They are in the home stretch of the journey, and their strong faith in the goodness and faithfulness of God remains a constant source of hope.

"Yea, though I walk through the valley of the shadow of death, I will fear no evil; For You are with me."

— Psalm 23:4

RECEIVING HELP AND GIVING HOPE

Hope is greater than a desire to live one more day. It is the belief that life has a higher purpose. The tapestry woven by a father and son illustrates this beautifully. Please consider this beautiful story of how the threads of the lives of a father and son wove one more picture on the tapestry they shared.

BRINGING HEALING BY RECEIVING CARE

Wayne was a college professor who loved to mentor his students. He enjoyed playing racquetball and tennis and setting the pace with students on back-packing trips into the local mountains.

Loss of balance sent him to the doctor initially. Multiple tests and expanding symptoms over the next two years led to a diagnosis of Progressive Supranuclear Palsy, an incurable and fatal disease that would ulti-mately leave him paralyzed and unable to read, eat, or speak. His life expectancy was cut to five years.

Wayne was a man of spiritual depth and conviction. He frequently and openly reflected on the qualities of love, self-sacrifice, and heroism, which he modeled in abundance. He was comfortable talking about spiri-tual things, including his personal relationship with Jesus Christ.

The progression of Wayne's disease made it more and more difficult for him to use his throat muscles to speak. However, he still seemed alert to conversations and activities around him. He could nod his head, track with his eyes, and laugh at the jokes.

The time came, though, when he could no longer swallow enough calories to survive. I thought that he would welcome the opportunity to end his life's trial because that is how I supposed I would feel. I would not want to suffer with a disease that trapped me in a useless body for the remainder of life.

I say "thought" because I have witnessed thousands of people executing Advance Health Directives. The vast majority of people check the box that states that, if death is imminent, they do not want to have a feeding tube inserted into their stomachs to provide artificial nutrition. I have sometimes wondered, when they were faced with the reality of imminent death, whether they would change their minds. Would I change my mind?

When Wayne was faced with that question, he chose life. We asked him "Do you want a feeding tube into your stomach?" He raised his finger up and down to indicate "Yes." Later, he gave the same response to the same question. Clearly he knew what was being asked, and he knew what he wanted to happen. Months earlier, we determined that Wayne wanted to move thousands of miles across the country to be near his only son, Ben.

After graduation from college, Ben had moved to his current home on the opposite side of the country. Although they communicated regularly, visits were very rare. Ben had not been there to walk with his family through the valley when his mother took an unplanned Safari and died of cancer.

Ben was eager to have his father move near him and found an adult family home a couple of miles from his home. Father and son relished their time together. Ben had a wheelchair ramp built over the stairs to his house, so he could bring his father to visit. They would watch football on the weekends. Ben often took Wayne to enjoy his favorite activity, fishing. Ben would bait and cast the hook and slide the rod down next to Wayne's wheelchair, so Wayne could "hold the rod." If he felt that familiar tug, Ben would reel in the fish "Dad had caught."

The feeding tube decision came after Wayne had been with his son for six months. Ben was pleased and relieved that his dad had chosen to extend his life with the use of the feeding tube. They had almost two years together after that time. There were a number of reunions, when Ben's sisters were able to join them. The time together was a second chance for Ben to re-connect with his father and to participate in the illness and death of a parent, a privilege that he had missed with his mother.

Did Wayne know that the time with his son would be so meaningful to Ben? I can't help but think that Wayne was being a hero. As he endured the pain and indignity of every day, he certainly knew there was a reason bigger than simply catching one more fish or just "stayin' alive." I believe that Wayne knew that Ben's soul was healing.

Wayne may also have known when the time was right and when the healing was done. After almost two and a half years with his son, with great effort and pain, Wayne pulled out his feeding tube. Ben took him to the hospital, where he died peacefully the next day.

On its face, this story seems to suggest that the self-sacrifice was only on the part of the loving son, Ben. But perhaps it is also a story of strength and sacrifice on the part of the father as well.

I had been surprised when I first heard that Wayne had chosen the feeding tube. However, after watching the story unfold, I believe that he was not trying to save himself; he was saving Ben. Wayne could not speak at the time, so we will never know for sure.

"Listen carefully: Unless a grain of wheat is buried in the ground, dead to the world, it is never any more than a grain of wheat. But if it is buried, it sprouts and reproduces itself many times over. In the same way, anyone who holds on to life just as it is destroys that life. But if you let it go, reckless in your love, you'll have it forever, real and eternal."

— John 12:24–25

WHEN LIFE ISN'T FAIR

I remember when I first became educated about the sport of NASCAR auto racing.

This is the way it works, or seems to work. Building up to the big race, some preliminary time trials are run to determine the starting position of the individual cars. At the start of the actual race, the cars line up two by two in a long line in the order of the fastest cars, based on the time trials, in the front of the pack. A pace car leads the race cars around the track, picking up speed as they go. As they approach the starting line, the pace car pulls off, the white flag drops, and the race begins.

At least it begins for the faster cars in front that are passing the starting line. The slower cars in the back are still moving their way up to the starting line to begin the race. The cars in the front are halfway around the track before the cars in the back have officially started the race. I ask you, "How is that fair?

It isn't fair, but it is real life. Some people are born at the head of the line and are flying through the starting gate with silver spoons in their mouths. Most, however, are running hard just to catch up, while a few others haven't yet received word that a race is even taking place.

We are all in the human race, and we will go around and around the track. It seems more "unfair" when we realize that some people will get their advertised 500 laps. And some will get far less than 500 laps. Their race will end sooner—their lives cut short in the prime of life or even earlier. Some will be doing many more than 500 laps—so many laps, at times, that they are praying that this turn in front of the grandstand will be their final lap.

The answer to the fairness question is what the answer has always been—the answer that Job received. God is in control of every molecule in the universe, and God loves me. He does all things well. He sees the sparrow fall, and He sees Grandma in the nursing home. God is on the Safari with you. Look for Him. He is there. Let me leave you with a story that serves as a reminder to me that God is in control in our lives. I hope it will serve you in that way as well.

GOD WINKS AS HE ANSWERS PRAYER

As my daughter and I were preparing for our trip to Africa, we met regularly with the other members of our team. Dave, one of the team members, offered a regular prayer request.

"My wife has an uncle who has been a missionary to Uganda for 40 years, and she has met him only when he came back to the states to visit. She lost contact with him after her mother passed away. Could we pray that I could meet up with him (Ron Devore) while we are in Africa, so my wife can reconnect with her uncle?"

We would pray regularly for Ron Devore and for Dave to be able to find him there. When we arrived in Uganda, Dave asked our guide if he could help us locate a missionary named Ron Devore. The guide explained that it would be quite impossible to find him, as the country had no telephone directories. Kampala, the capital city, held more than 3 million people and had no method of tracking people. He said that unless Dave had Ron Devore's phone number or address, it would be impossible to try to locate him. There was just no method to make contact.

The next day our team was having lunch at a large covered shopping area. My daughter happened to be wearing a t-shirt that had the name of our hometown (Poulsbo) in large letters on the front. As we were moving toward a table to be seated, someone in a group of about 10 people off to our left said, loud enough for all of us to hear, "Poulsbo, I know Poulsbo." I walked over to introduce myself and hear his story.

He was from Renton, Washington, a city about 60 miles from Poulsbo, and he was visiting Uganda to attend a conference conducted every year by a certain missionary. He pointed with his thumb to the man sitting next to him as he said his name, Ron Devore!

Can you believe it? In a city of three million people, a man recognized the name on a shirt that my daughter happened to be wearing. He called out, and I spoke with him. Wow. Coincidence? Not on your life! Do not tell me that God is not in control. I tell this story as a small illustration of our awesome God and His ability to connect the dots of our lives. We were on this journey in a distant land, and God saw fit to answer our prayer.

Live in the hope that all things are in His hands. Many Accidental Safaris require such a high level of care for the patient that the focus is beyond the ability of a loved one to provide, beyond the ability of a family to provide, or maybe even beyond the skill of a professional caregiver.

As you face the battles in your life, at whatever stage, whatever phase, whether life or death, the God of the universe is also the God of your situation. Every molecule moves at His permission. He is in charge and loves you. Your insufficiency to face your crisis is the greatest proof that Jesus will be the abundance needed to see you through to the glorious end He has prepared for you. A relationship with Jesus does not provide protection from the Safaris of life, but He promises that His presence will never leave us. I can think of no better guide through all the journeys of this life. Never lose hope.

APPENDIX

38 CFR § 3.2 PERIODS OF WAR

This section sets forth the beginning and ending dates of each war period beginning with the Indian wars. Note that the term *period of war* in reference to pension entitlement under 38 U.S.C. 1521, 1541 and 1542 means all of the war periods listed in this section except the Indian wars and the Spanish-American War. See § 3.3(a)(3) and (b)(4)(i).

a. *Indian wars.* January 1, 1817, through December 31, 1898, inclusive. Service must have been rendered with the United States military forces against Indian tribes or nations.

b. *Spanish-American War.* April 21, 1898, through July 4, 1902, inclusive. If the veteran served with the United States military forces engaged in hostilities in the Moro Province, the ending date is July 15, 1903. The Philippine Insurrection and the Boxer Rebellion are included.

c. *World War I.* April 6, 1917, through November 11, 1918, inclusive. If the veteran served with the United States military forces in Russia, the ending date is April 1, 1920. Service after November 11, 1918, and before July 2, 1921, is considered World War I service if the veteran served in the active military, naval, or air service after April 5, 1917, and before November 12, 1918.

d. *World War II.* December 7, 1941, through December 31, 1946, inclusive. If the veteran was in service on December 31, 1946, continuous service before July 26, 1947, is considered World War II service.

e. *Korean conflict.* June 27, 1950, through January 31, 1955, inclusive.

f. *Vietnam era.* The period beginning on February 28, 1961, and ending on May 7, 1975, inclusive, in the case of a veteran who served in the Republic of Vietnam during that period. The period beginning on August 5, 1964, and ending on May 7, 1975, inclusive, in all other cases.

(Authority: 38 U.S.C. 101(29))

g. *Future dates.* The period beginning on the date of any future declaration of war by the Congress and ending on a date prescribed by Presidential proclamation or concurrent resolution of the Congress.

(Authority: 38 U.S.C. 101)

h. *Mexican border period.* May 9, 1916, through April 5, 1917, in the case of a veteran who during such period served in Mexico, on the borders thereof, or in the waters adjacent thereto.

(Authority: 38 U.S.C. 101(30))

i. Persian Gulf War. August 2, 1990, through date to be prescribed by Presidential proclamation or law.

(Authority: 38 U.S.C. 101(33))

[26 FR 1563, Feb. 24, 1961, as amended at 32 FR 13223, Sept. 19, 1967; 36 FR 8445, May 6, 1971; 37 FR 6676, Apr. 1, 1972; 40 FR 27030, June 26, 1975; 44 FR 45931, Aug. 6, 1979; 56 FR 57986, Nov. 15, 1991; 62 FR 35422, July 1, 1997]

ENDNOTES

1. A.H. Greenhouse, "Falls among the elderly." In: M.L. Albert and J.E. Knoefel, Eds. *Clinical neurology of aging*. 2nd ed. New York: Oxford University Press, 1994, 611–26, cited in Fuller, George F. Fuller, "Falls in the Elderly." American Family Physician, April 1, 2000,61(7), 2159-2168. Retrieved from <http://www.aafp.org/afp/2000/0401/p2159.html>.

2. CDC/NCHS. National Vital Statistics System, Mortality, cited in Ellen Kramarow, Li-Hui Chen, Holly Hedegaard, and Margaret Warner, May 2015. "Deaths From Unintentional Injury Among Adults Aged 65 and Over: United States, 2000–2013. " National Center for Health Statistics. NCHS Data Brief No. 199. Retrieved from <https://www.cdc.gov/nchs/data/databriefs/db199.htm>.

3. "Suicide in the Elderly." American Association for Marriage and Family Therapy, 2017. Retrieved from

<http://www.aamft.org/iMIS15/AAMFT/Content/
Consumer_Updates/Suicide_in_the_Elderly.aspx>.

4. Robert Pear. "New Medicare Law to Notify Patients of
    Loophole in Nursing Home Coverage." *The New York
    Times*, August 6, 2016. Retrieved from <https://www.
    nytimes.com/2016/08/07/us/politics/new-medicare-
    law-to-notify-patients-of-loophole-in-nursing-home-
    coverage.html>.

5. Jeannette Belliveau, 2017. "Signs and Symptoms
    of Ministroke." Healthline Media. Retrieved
    from <http://www.healthline.com/health/stroke/
    signs-symptoms-tia-mini-stroke#Whatisaministroke?1>.

6. "Self-Help Packet for Skilled Nursing Facility Appeals
    Including 'Improvement Standard' Denials." Center for
    Medicare Advocacy, 2015. Retrieved from <http://www.
    medicareadvocacy.org/self-help-packet-for-expedited-
    skilled-nursing-facility-appeals-including-improvement-
    standard-denials/>.

7. "Self Help Materials." Center for Medicare
    Advocacy, 2015. Retrieved from <http://
    www.medicareadvocacy.org/take-action/
    self-help-packets-for-medicare-appeals/>.

8. L. Ganzini et al., July 24, 2003. "Nurses' experiences
    with hospice patients who refuse food and fluids to
    hasten death." *New England Journal of Medicine*; 349(4):
    359-65. Retrieved from PubMed.gov <https://www.
    ncbi.nlm.nih.gov/pubmed/12878744>.

9.   "Who Needs Care?" (September 25, 2017). U.S. Department of Health and Human Services. Retrieved from LongTemCare.gov at <http://longtermcare.gov/the-basics/who-needs-care.html>.

10.   Revised Code of Washington (RCW). Title 68, Chapter 68.50, Section 68.50.160. Retrieved from <http://app.leg.wa.gov/RCW/default.aspx?cite=68.50.160>.

11.   "Long-term-care insurance: Insurers are forced to boost premiums or stop selling policies." Consumer Reports Money Adviser, August 2012. Retrieved from <https://www.consumerreports.org/cro/2012/08/long-term-care-insurance/index.htm>.

12.   "Veterans' Diseases Associated with Agent Orange." U.S. Department of Veterans Affairs, June 3, 2015). Retrieved from <https://www.publichealth.va.gov/exposures/agentorange/conditions/>.

13.   "Sixty-Five Plus in the United States." U.S. Census Bureau: Statistical Brief, May 1995. Economics and Statistics Administration, U.S. Department of Commerce. Retrieved from https://www.census.gov/population/socdemo/statbriefs/agebrief.html.

14.   See note 13 above.

15.   See note 13 above.

16.   "Elderly Abuse Statistics." Statistic Brain Research Institute, 2017. Retrieved from http://www.statistic-brain.com/elderly-abuse-statistics/.

17.   "Misuse of Prescription Drugs." National Institute on Drug Abuse: Research Report Series, August

2016. Retrieved from <https://www.drugabuse.gov/publications/research-reports/prescription-drugs/trends-in-prescription-drug-abuse/older-adults>.

18. "Elder or Dependent Adult Neglect" *Psychology Today*, May 18, 2017. Health Profs.com. Retrieved from <https://www.psychologytoday.com/conditions/elder-or-dependent-adult-neglect>.

19. Robyn Dixon. "I Will Eat Your Dollars." *Los Angeles Times*, October 20, 2005. Retrieved June 22, 2012. Retrieved from <https://en.wikipedia.org/wiki/Advance-fee_scam>.

REFERENCES

Belliveau, Jeannette, 2017."Signs and Symptoms of Ministroke." Healthline Media. Retrieved from <http://www.healthline.com/health/stroke/ signs-symptoms-tia-mini-stroke#Whatisaministroke?1>.

CDC/NCHS. National Vital Statistics System, Mortality, cited in Kramarow E.; , Chen,L.H.; Hedegaard,H.; and Warner, M. May 2015. "Deaths From Unintentional Injury Among Adults Aged 65 and Over: United States, 2000–2013. " National Center for Health Statistics. NCHS Data Brief No. 199. Retrieved from <https:// www.cdc.gov/nchs/data/databriefs/db199.htm>.

Dixon, Robyn. "I Will Eat Your Dollars." *Los Angeles Times,* October 20, 2005. Retrieved June 22, 2012. Retrieved from <https://en.wikipedia.org/wiki/ Advance-fee_scam>.

"Elderly Abuse Statistics." Statistic Brain Research Institute, 2017. Retrieved from http://www.statisticbrain.com/elderly-abuse-statistics/.

"Elder or Dependent Adult Neglect" *Psychology Today*, May 18, 2017. Health Profs.com. Retrieved from <https://www.psychologytoday.com/conditions/elder-or-dependent-adult-neglect>.

Ganzini, L.; Goy, E.R.; Miller, L.L.; Harvath, T.A.; Jackson, A.; and Delorit, M.A. July 24, 2003. "Nurses' experiences with hospice patients who refuse food and fluids to hasten death." *New England Journal of Medicine*; 349(4): 359-65. Retrieved from PubMed.gov

<https://www.ncbi.nlm.nih.gov/pubmed/12878744>.

Greenhouse, A.H. "Falls among the elderly." In: Albert, M.L. and Knoefel, J.E., Eds. *Clinical neurology of aging*. 2nd ed. New York: Oxford University Press, 1994, 611–26, cited in Fuller, George F. Fuller, "Falls in the Elderly." American Family Physician, April 1, 2000,61(7), 2159-2168. Retrieved from <http://www.aafp.org/afp/2000/0401/p2159.html>.

"Long-term-care insurance: Insurers are forced to boost premiums or stop selling policies." Consumer Reports Money Adviser, August 2012. Retrieved from <https://www.consumerreports.org/cro/2012/08/long-term-care-insurance/index.htm>.

"Misuse of Prescription Drugs." National Institute on Drug Abuse: Research Report Series, August 2016. Retrieved from <https://www.drugabuse.gov/

publications/research-reports/prescription-drugs/
trends-in-prescription-drug-abuse/older-adults>.

Pear, Robert. "New Medicare Law to Notify Patients of Loophole in Nursing Home Coverage." *The New York Times*, August 6, 2016. Retrieved from <https://www.nytimes.com/2016/08/07/us/politics/new-medicare-law-to-notify-patients-of-loophole-in-nursing-home-coverage.html>.

Revised Code of Washington (RCW). Title 68, Chapter 68.50, Section 68.50.160. Retrieved from <http://app.leg.wa.gov/RCW/default.aspx?cite=68.50.160>.

"Self-Help Packet for Skilled Nursing Facility Appeals Including 'Improvement Standard' Denials." Center for Medicare Advocacy, 2015. Retrieved from <http://www.medicareadvocacy.org/self-help-packet-for-expedited-skilled-nursing-facility-appeals-including-improvement-standard-denials/>.

"Self Help Materials." Center for Medicare Advocacy, 2015. Retrieved from <http://www.medicareadvocacy.org/take-action/self-help-packets-for-medicare-appeals/>.

"Sixty-Five Plus in the United States." U.S. Census Bureau: Statistical Brief, May 1995. Economics and Statistics Administration, U.S. Department of Commerce. Retrieved from https://www.census.gov/population/socdemo/statbriefs/agebrief.html.

"Suicide in the Elderly." American Association for Marriage and Family Therapy, 2017. Retrieved from <http://

www.aamft.org/iMIS15/AAMFT/Content/Consumer_
Updates/Suicide_in_the_Elderly.aspx>.

Veterans' Diseases Associated with Agent Orange." U.S.
Department of Veterans Affairs, June 3, 2015).
Retrieved from <https://www.publichealth.va.gov/
exposures/agentorange/conditions/>.

Who Needs Care?" (September 25, 2017). U.S. Department
of Health and Human Services. Retrieved from
LongTemCare.gov at <http://longtermcare.gov/the-
basics/who-needs-care.html>.

CPSIA information can be obtained
at www.ICGtesting.com
Printed in the USA
LVHW041512040919
629924LV00012B/1104